EXAGGERATED CLAIMS?

SAGE SWIFTS

In 1976 SAGE published a series of short 'university papers', which led to the publication of the QASS series (or the 'little green books' as they became known to researchers). Almost 40 years since the release of the first 'little green book', SAGE is delighted to offer a new series of swift, short and topical pieces in the ever-growing digital environment.

SAGE *Swifts* offer authors a new channel for academic research with the freedom to deliver work outside the conventional length of journal articles. The series aims to give authors speedy access to academic audiences through digital first publication, space to explore ideas thoroughly, yet at a length which can be readily digested, and the quality stamp and reassurance of peer-review.

EXAGGERATED CLAIMS?

THE ESRC, 50 YEARS ON

DAVID WALKER

Los Angeles | London | New Delhi
Singapore | Washington DC

Los Angeles | London | New Delhi
Singapore | Washington DC

SAGE Publications Ltd
1 Oliver's Yard
55 City Road
London EC1Y 1SP

SAGE Publications Inc.
2455 Teller Road
Thousand Oaks, California 91320

SAGE Publications India Pvt Ltd
B 1/I 1 Mohan Cooperative Industrial Area
Mathura Road
New Delhi 110 044

SAGE Publications Asia-Pacific Pte Ltd
3 Church Street
#10-04 Samsung Hub
Singapore 049483

Editor: Chris Rojek
Editorial assistant: Delayna Spencer
Production editor: Vanessa Harwood
Marketing manager: Michael Ainsley
Cover design: Jen Crisp
Typeset by: C&M Digitals (P) Ltd, Chennai, India
Printed and bound by CPI Group (UK) Ltd,
Croydon, CR0 4YY

© David Walker 2016

First published 2016

Library of Congress Control Number: 2015954635

British Library Cataloguing in Publication data

A catalogue record for this book is available from
the British Library

ISBN 978-1-4739-4223-3
eISBN 978-1-4739-6702-1

CONTENTS

About the Author   vi
Preface   vii

1 Introduction   1

2 The ESRC Today   16

3 Promise and Disappointment   36

4 Reprieve and Normalisation   49

5 An Agent of Amelioration   59

6 Academic Capture   71

7 Cumulative Knowledge?   83

8 Conclusion   98

References   109
Index   117

ABOUT THE AUTHOR

David Walker is Head of Policy for the Academy of Social Sciences. For seven years he was Chair of the ESRC Methods and Infrastructure Committee, after seven years on ESRC Council. He is Chair of the governing board for Understanding Society and a member of UK Biobank Ethics and Governance Committee.

During a career in journalism and public affairs, he worked for *The Times Higher Education Supplement*, *The Economist*, *The Times*, the BBC and the *Guardian*, where he was founding editor of *Public* magazine.

His books include *Cameron's Coup* co-written with Polly Toynbee (Guardian Faber Publishing, 2015), *The Verdict* (Granta, 2010), *Unjust Rewards* (Granta, 2008), *Sources Close to the Prime Minister* with Peter Hennessy and Michael Cockerell (MacMillan, 1985) and *Media Made in California* with Jeremy Tunstall (Oxford University Press, 1981).

PREFACE

This is in part a labour of autobiography, using my own cuttings from *The Times Higher Education Supplement* (where I was once social sciences correspondent) and contributions to *New Society, The Times, Guardian* and other media. I also declare an old financial interest. As holder of an SSRC Studentship I did a master's but, along with many others at the time, then failed to complete a PhD – to the topic of which neither my supervisor nor the SSRC paid the least attention. So I added in a small way to the political pressure on the SSRC mounting from the late 1970s onwards. I can bring empathy to the SSRC's survival as a friendless quango, having worked at the Audit Commission when its doom was pronounced by the Cameron government, albeit by a Tory minister less intellectually complex than the SSRC's nemesis, Sir Keith Joseph.

To make amends for squandering my studentship I have over the years contributed time and enthusiasm to ESRC projects, as a serial member of advisory committees then, from 2006, a member of the Council itself. On it, I first chaired the Information Committee, then the Research Resources Board, which became the Methods and Infrastructure Committee. This is, however, in no way an official project. The ESRC has known about it, but that is all. I acknowledge the assistance of Jacky Clake, head of information, in providing material from the archive at Swindon.

I would like to dedicate the book to Sharon, Jane and Tessa, who demonstrate that whatever commitments a social scientist takes on, in government, organisational life and academe, she retains the capacity to hold roles and institutional settings at an analytical distance.

I
INTRODUCTION

SUMMARY

In 50 years the UK's social science research funder has paid for prodigious amounts of knowledge. But 'for whom' and 'for what' are questions too rarely posed since its birth in the optimistic social democratic circumstances of the mid-1960s. Its history pivots around producing knowledge that passes muster among academics in their disciplines and expecting social science research to address specific problems in economy and society. At its birth, warnings were heard about 'exaggerated claims' by the social sciences. They were prescient. The knowledge it pays for is, often, antinomian, autistic and disconnected from the rest of the state's apparatus for generating socio-economic insight.

If you believe academics are disinterested seekers after knowledge, this book may annoy you. If you see universities as repositories of truth and their work self-justifying, the sceptical tone may offend.

If you believe disciplinary knowledge should be reserved for the initiated (their PhD a minimal requirement to voice opinions on internal matters), you will cry trespass. My adage comes from the distinguished American applied social scientist Richard Nathan. The conduct of social science research is not only a matter of what social science can do for the real world. It is also very much a matter of what the real world can do for social science (Nathan, 1998).

An account of the 50 years of the UK's research council for social science is inescapably about universities. And so it's about the research commissioners' impotence over trends both within universities and the higher education system: massification, bureaucratisation, intensification of specialisation and the incompatibility of subject departments and dedicated (preferably multidisciplinary) research centres and units. It did not have to be. Those who willed the council into existence thought it should be more than a facilitator of work by academics.

The knowledge they believed the UK needed could and should be produced plurally, even competitively in freestanding research centres, even in-house. Within a few years they admitted defeat. The subsequent history shows the tensions between academics producing knowledge that passes muster in their disciplines and those (ministers, MPs, media, think tanks, interest groups, business firms) who expect social science research to address the problems they confront. How knowledge is labelled is usually irrelevant to them; what matters is its utility and applicability – which academics think jeopardise their autonomy in defining what knowledge is. By autonomy they mean monopoly. Problems, societal issues, grand challenges – whatever we call them – 'are essentially public ones'; they ought 'to be debated in hybrid in which there is no entrance ticket in terms of expertise' (Gibbons et al., 1994: 148). Wishful thinking; these authors (including the protean Martin Trow) dreamt of 'participatory science' where 'the goal is no longer truth per se but responsible public decision making based upon understanding complex situations where many key uncertainties remain to be resolved'. Reaching that goal would take demolition of much of the apparatus of academic knowledge production – and a cognitive revolution on the part of the state: both are above the research council's pay grade.

What to call this quango, which survived assassination in the 1980s only by shape shifting from the Social Science Research Council to a new identity as the Economic and Social Research Council? What's in a name? A lot: retreat from a wider, continuous conversation about social science that such a body, if anyone, should carry; intellectual thraldom to one discipline, economics, rendering its ideology, its omissions and its pretensions off limits. Here, let's abbreviate and call it *the Council* except in explicit pre- and post-1984 contexts.

Another problem is Macavity. As the knowledge economy changed, it often seemed the Council wasn't there. But because there was (and remains) nobody else to voice social science as a collective endeavour, it went unspoken. The print of the UK government's other agencies for social science was usually also hard to detect, including the Central Statistical Office and the Office of Population Censuses and Surveys (now the Office of National Statistics), research committees inside government departments, the Bank of England and so on. The Council's non-relationship with these other bodies is looked at in Chapter 2.

Silence may be the fate of research funders, in the middle, squeezed between disciplines, universities and academics on the one side and government, decision makers, media and society on the other; their 'brand' is fated to be pallid. It took a long time for the Council to define its purposes and even now there remains ambiguity about its mission – bound up with issues of cognitive hierarchy and epistemology. As for 'representation' of the activity doing social science it

> cannot be a spokesperson … because it has simultaneously to represent the merits of social sciences research to its paymaster, regulate what is acceptable in much of the research, allocate government's money and ensure good value for the public funds which it allocates … it is not independent enough of government to provide the necessary advice. (Commission on the Social Sciences, 2003: 105)

These points need unpacking (see Chapters 2 and 6). Here, let's note the ESRC's logo for 2015 says '50 years shaping society' and agree two things:

1. Knowledge has causal strength. States have believed this for centuries, which is why control of data and information are such persistent themes. The UK state evidently believes it, for how else to explain the enforcement on the ESRC of 'purdah', during the 2015 UK general election or, in September 2014, the Scottish independence referendum? Universities and research units are not banned from publicising findings in the weeks before elections or referendums provided they 'avoid reference to the ESRC as a source of the funding'. Anonymous knowledge is permitted; knowledge produced by a government body (whose raison d'être is knowledge production) is not.
2. The way social science knowledge does 'shape society' – exert any causality – is barely understood. It is the subject of assertion, rhetoric and assumption, but despite recent fuss about impact, few social scientists or the Council have bothered much with the sociology of research-generated knowledge. This is a history from which self-reflexivity is largely absent. Metaphors abound to capture the ways knowledge enters consciousness (unconsciously) but empirical studies, even retrospective 'Agatha Christie' narratives in which actors are asked what they knew and when, are few and far between. How many times writers lazily cite that passage from Keynes about decision makers in business catching something from the air that in fact stems from 'academic scribblers' way back. Is knowledge really so evanescent, the history of ideas so impenetrable that we can't get a better grip on how much and how far yesterday's research may still be present today? Perhaps – heretical thought – social science knowledge is only fitfully cumulative; it is instead episodic, context-dependent, specific to institutions, immanent – not (as 'science' believes) transcendent. More in Chapter 7.

PRODIGIOUS GROWTH

Most indices show the expansion of knowledge over the half-century. Not all. The proportion of GDP spent on research and development has dropped, from 2.3 per cent in 1965 to around 1.7 per cent in 2014. But since 1965 Council spending on social science has outstripped growth in GDP by about three to one. From just over 2 per cent of total research council spending 50 years ago, the ESRC now gets 6 per cent. Growth in the 'products of knowledge' has been tumultuous. To take only one discipline, sociology, since the 1960s the professional association has created three new journals; to them should be added many commercially published journals, in the UK and abroad. A telling sign of the intensification of specialist knowledge is the increase in the ratio of papers given at conferences to attendance at them, rising from 9 per cent in 1965 to 55 per cent at the turn of the century (Platt, 2003: 53). Postgraduate numbers have risen along with social science staff in UK universities, though accounting is made difficult because people are doing social science under a variety of labels, including business and health. The estimated value of social science research from all sources – university grants, research council, foundations, government departments, etc. – has grown from £120 million in the mid-1960s by at least a factor of five. Incidental improvements include the productivity of Council staff, measured both by total spending per head and grants awarded per head (neither of which, like most statements about public sector productivity, are especially meaningful).

By the late 1970s, observers extolled the 'sheer volume of research and publication ... units, groups, teams, serviced by an infrastructure of information and computing beyond the imaginings of a mere 25 years ago' (Cherns, 1979: 86). The point could be made today about the past quarter-century. But what relationship does the vast outpouring of books, articles, blogs, papers, presentations by academic social scientists – some of it paid for through the Council, but not always identifiable as such – have to decision making, understanding and daily practice in institutions, households or by individuals? There you have the 'impact' question, which in various guises will tease us through this book. Efforts to answer it made by the ESRC and the funders of higher education are both puny and strangely recent. For years, it seems, academics have researched, grants have been awarded, university departments shrunk and expanded without much evidence or even curiosity about whether the knowledge being generated was available (to other than its authors), let alone informing understanding or behaviour. The Heyworth Committee asked the question, its secretary reported, but received no satisfactory answers. It was clear that the actual processes whereby research influenced action were not well understood either by researchers or by administrators. Nor were they aware that they did not know that there was any problem. Time and again a line of questioning by Heyworth evoked blank incomprehension. (Cherns, 1969: 122)

ANTINOMIAN KNOWLEDGE

Social self-knowledge veers towards the antinomian, which Daniel Bell once cited among the cultural contradictions of capitalism (Bell, 1972). Put the point another way. 'Users' are magpies. They don't know where this piece of intelligence/concept/perception comes from, but if it suits their material purpose, they will put it to use. *Academic* knowledge demands certification; academics are celebrants at the cult of the reference. *Action* has to be cognitively eclectic. Here is a recipe for perennial tension between 'evidence' (as academics see it) and executive decision. Where does the Council fit? Is it a mere underlabourer, providing the money so the academics can attest to the quality of the knowledge they produce, or should it side with the users in their eclecticism? Its administrative fate (a choice necessitated by the strength of the universities and the peculiar indifference of the UK state towards data and analysis) has been the former.

This picture is too Manichean, some might say: users can cohabit with academics. This is the official view. 'User inputs feed in at several different levels – the setting of priority themes, selection of new programmes' (Alsop, 1999: 12). But 'the ESRC is careful to ensure that the input of users into assessment does not become a diktat on agenda, methods or outcome' (Alsop, 1999: 12). But what, in this view, is the nature of the conversation between user and producer: is it mutually respectful, epistemologically egalitarian? What actually takes place – if it takes place – is rarely that.

Knowledge for and in government is diverse and undifferentiated. For example, the ESRC supports research on retailing. It says it has helped transform thinking (ESRC, 2014a). The Cameron coalition said it cared about the high street and, though it disliked overt intervention in markets, expressed an interest in shops; Mary Portas was appointed retail tsar. In October 2013 BIS produced a Strategy for Future Retail (BIS, 2013). The knowledge base would be provided by BIS itself, retail sector bodies, retailers, the retail sector skills council and … the research councils. No hierarchy. No cognitive privilege. All hands to the pumps. In the eyes of users (in this instance, the Whitehall department responsible for the ESRC) knowledge attested by the research bodies is not prime.

Another example. The Magenta Book (HM Treasury, 2011) offers officials in-depth guidance on how evaluation should be designed and undertaken. The treatise acknowledges the ESRC, its data sets and work on research methods. These belong to the 'infrastructure' of social knowledge, which the ESRC supports. So the Council is visible, but how *central*? It's a player, but one among several; ONS and the Bank of England also support the socio-economic knowledge infrastructure. The government itself collects and analyses socio-economic data, which it analyses in-house and through semi-independent agencies such as the Office for Budget Responsibility. It's not clear what the division of labour might be between various knowledge organisations or whether the knowledge user/disseminator (HM Treasury) particularly cares.

This is more than a rehash of where to locate the boundary between 'fundamental' and applied work. The Treasury reputedly relied on ESRC-supported theoretical work on auctions when it sold off G3 spectrum, allowing one of the academics involved somewhat immodestly to claim the financial gains would pay for public spending on social science for years (Binmore, 2003: xviii). But if (as some say) there is only knowledge awaiting use and knowledge in use, academics will assert command of the criteria for allocating support, for only they know what is 'interesting'.

The Magenta Book mentions an econometric evaluation of the Labour government's New Deal programme; it's a sophisticated piece of social science work (DWP, 2003). This is knowledge in use. Would the ESRC have made a grant for something similar? Or is its role in the basement of the edifice, assuming systemic responsibility for the quality of the social science employed? It doesn't seem so. 'We are concerned about the future capacity for research outside universities given the academic focus of ESRC-funded research training', the Commission on the Social Sciences concluded (Commission on the Social Sciences, 2003: 8). There is a community of applied researchers, even a proto-professional body (the Social Research Association). If these bodies police standards and enforce quality control, the ESRC is not readily identifiable as a coadjutor.

If there is a UK social science *system*, it is disarticulated and nobody, certainly not the research council, oversees or lubricates it, except through regulating the flow of social science postgraduates and certain limited interventions in universities, offering opportunities to researchers. If Sharon Witherspoon, former director of the Nuffield Foundation, is right and there is a deficiency in funding work in between the data infrastructure and practice, whose concern should that be (Witherspoon, 2015)? Who inspects how research findings at large get communicated to policy makers and their intellectual standards? Do we treat as equivalent a story from a public relations firm offering the findings from a survey of 100 people and a research report emanating from a properly weighted sample survey involving thousands? Who should apply tests and quality control if not a social science research council?

SOCIAL SCIENCE RESEARCH – WHAT DO WE KNOW?

The Council and its processes for knowledge production have barely been studied. We need more research on research (Wilsdon et al., 2015) because in self-reflexivity lies the basis of strategy. The study of research systems is poorly funded in the UK. Here's a causal proposition: different (research) workplaces promote different (social) science. It was worth exploring in the 1970s when the state of knowledge concerning even the basic parameters and dynamics of social science research organisations was pronounced rudimentary (Crawford and Perry, 1976: 9). The proposition remains as worthy of testing now as then. We need institutional analysis, history and – in the case of the Council – more debate about purpose and process. During the Council's first decade it instigated and contributed to debate about the division of labour between knowledge bodies; it no longer takes that system-wide view. The missing history need not be bland. Across the postwar social science scene stride some big personalities, for example the late Claus Moser, statistician, civil servant, trustee, think tanker, panjandrum: a biography is lacking.

A barrier to tracing impact from research into policy and practice is 'lack of information on interactions between researchers and users' (ESRC, 2013a: 8). Once, the Council was urged to focus on social science utilisation, and upgrading the 'use capacity' of organisations (Cherns, 1972); it did not happen. On a key question – whether research support (through the Council) does indeed shape knowledge – we lack evidence. Colin Talbot did something unusual: he asked civil servants where they looked for knowledge. They value general expertise as much, or more, than they do specific research (Talbot and Talbot, 2014).

It's not just the Council. Other agencies potentially important in structuring knowledge are as unknown, among them the learned societies and the disciplinary clubs. They seem important as gatekeepers, undergirding peer review and the activities of both the Council and the higher education funding agencies, yet are notoriously under-financed, and habitually dependent on the donated time of a few active disciplinarians. They have become structurally weaker, anyway. 'Collegial bodies are (now) given less account than individual higher education institutions that no longer have "care" for the overall research eco system rather than their individual positioning within it' (BSA, 2014: 1). One of my themes is how early synoptic or interdisciplinary ambitions were thwarted. 'Despite encouragement from the ESRC, work that analyses problems in a multidisciplinary way is relatively unusual', reports the former head of government social research (Duncan, 2015). The story is about how social science was tracked into tightly bounded disciplines; why the SSRC was powerless to intervene when entire disciplines – sociology, later economics – went astray ('astray' in terms of the original mission of the Council; the only other non-teleological sense of 'astray' is movement away from providing general understanding of social and economic conditions). Put that another way: peer review dominated disciplines but *social science* could muster no peers, no generic practitioners. Institutionally social science in the UK was and remains weak. National bodies such as the British Academy and the Royal Society of Edinburgh either came late to 'representation' of social science or offer that only fitfully.

THE INVISIBLE ESRC

'The ESRC is perceived as "quiet"' (ESRC, 2013b). An organisation dedicated to public enlightenment (we hope) is barely known to the public. Are citizens its 'customers'? Does it matter that the funding body goes unseen if the work it supports gets picked up? A science purist would say no: labelling does not matter. In the real world of budgets and lobbying for exiguous funds, it does.

Even in the pitted, hill-and-dale landscape of British public bodies, the Council is oddly elusive. In the early 1980s it gave academics, along with William Plowden, then Director General of the Royal Institute of Public Administration, a grant to examine the Joint Approach to Social Policy (JASP), a 1970s effort instigated by the Central Policy Review Staff to combat the fragmentation of Whitehall departments and local government. The initiative failed, only to be resurrected in various guises – cabinet committees and the like – over subsequent years. The story of JASP is, in part, about what the state knows. Yet the write-up doesn't mention the knowledge body that gave them the money, either as an actor or reference point (Challis et al., 1988). This account of an attempt to push rationality as an organising principle of government discussed the creation of the Department of Economic Affairs, the Fulton Report, the arrival of cost-benefit analysis, the commissions on local government, the reorganisation of the NHS (by Keith Joseph, the SSRC's nemesis), but not a word about the SSRC – even though one of its champions under the Wilson government of 1966–70, Shirley Williams, became chair of the 'strategic' group of ministers overseeing JASP in the Wilson government of 1974–6. This may be a reflection of a generic indifference to knowledge and expertise in Whitehall.

The CPRS was called 'the think tank' but was a nest of dilettantes and 'bright young things' rather than experts: their skills were those of consultants, marshalling what evidence there was and reaching recommendations (Bulmer, 1987: 17). Even so, the absence is striking, especially (as we see in Chapter 3) because the SSRC's leadership was anxious at the time to up its influence.

Another illustrative non-appearance by Macavity is in an analysis by the House of Commons Library (House of Commons Library, 2015) of Sure Start, a high-profile social intervention that survived Labour's exit from power in 2010, but has since been cut back. High hopes and political suspicion swirl around it, as an instrument to advance social mobility and improve the life chances of poor children. It touches on big social science themes to do with background and inter-generational continuity in disadvantage. The Library's summary relied heavily on Sir John Hills and colleagues at the LSE Centre for Analysis of Social Exclusion (CASE, 2015). CASE has passed in and out of ESRC sponsorship. Why it did not become a flagship 'IFS for social policy' is unclear unless, as with IFS, academic jealousies have played a dispiriting role, together with hesitation on the part of the Council about long-term funding of centres and units – stemming from its uncertain sociology of social science knowledge production. Significantly, the ESRC did not sponsor CASE's audit of coalition social policy, which was paid for by the Joseph Rowntree Foundation, the Trust for London and the Nuffield Foundation.

This practical evaluation is social science in action. Hills is one of the country's most eminent students of poverty, housing and inequality. Several disciplinary lines weave through the genealogy of policies and political commitments in Sure Start. Ideas from the United States, previous social science research, ministerial instincts about early years interventions: they all play a part. What's hard, perhaps impossible, to sift are specific connections between discrete pieces of research, academic journals, analysis by governments and outcomes, including (we hope) better lives for children. Associations, yes; causation, no. Science but no precision. Instincts are as important as (rare and peripheral) randomised controlled trials. Distinguishing the Council's part is hard, perhaps impossible. This book will use the simile of a pool or lake, which is borrowed from Janet Lewis, former research director of the Joseph Rowntree Foundation. Over 50 years the Council has pumped kilolitres into it but has little idea – who has? – about how or when abstraction occurs, who bathes, and who avoids the water altogether. When we see an instance of paddling, we know little about what, cognitively speaking, is going on. In the University of Cambridge's submissions to the 2014 REF impact exercise (Impact Case Study REF 3b), ESRC research was cited and impact was registered by the researcher's receipt of a letter from David Willetts (before he became science minister in the Cameron coalition). In it he attested to his interest in the research, saying: 'I am trying to make sense of the debate about the extent to which attitudes are shaped by the cohorts to which people belong or by stage in the life cycle'. The researcher was praised for her 'interesting and valuable' study. Willetts (writing his own book about intergenerational transfers and justice) would have been remiss not to find the research interesting because he too is swimming or paddling and the waves of knowledge are breaking; but is this 'engagement' or 'impact', let alone 'transfer'?

The background role played by the Council is of a piece with the pluriform and often unpredictable course that knowledge for government takes. Of course statecraft is immersed in 'evidence' – meaning analysis, modelling, the deployment of information and data. But government welcomes expertise and research findings only in doses, and fitfully at that. The introduction to George Osborne's 2015 spending review (HM Treasury, 2015) is a prime exhibit. It makes no explicit mention of evidence or data, let alone research or science, social or otherwise. The victorious Tory party knows what it wants; it has a Commons majority; who is going to reprimand it for non-sequiturs or unsubstantiated assertion? The document does cite data collected by government departments, the ONS, Office of Budget Responsibility and think tanks (the King's Fund). Also 'expertise' is to be tapped, it says, from the 'What Works' centres, established with the support of the ESRC (see Chapter 2).

These centres exemplify the problem described above. They cross and recross between science (what academics do for its own sake), evaluation and practical analysis. The ESRC tries to throw a blanket over the whole, saying it only supports 'excellence'. What that means in practice is knowledge generated and attested within academic circuits, peer review by the established disciplines.

AUTISTIC KNOWLEDGE

Peer-reviewed, 'disciplined', unchallengeable from outside the college: these became hallmarks of the knowledge supported by the Council. Its history revolves around the over-production of autistic knowledge. The first chair of the SSRC, Michael Young, believed that social science research would produce knowledge that decision makers would absorb and – the Enlightenment nostrum – in knowing more, they would make better decisions. Within a few years of its foundation the Council had moved away from anything as straightforward. It moved to support research without any purchase on what happened to it, becoming an intermediary between government and what came to be called the community of social scientists. Except the professors weren't solidaristic: they tended to put discipline before the common weal. After a decade the former secretary to the Heyworth Committee found the social science disciplines 'lead separate lives' (Cherns, 1979: 26). They come together only under the umbrella of the SSRC, in a few multidisciplinary institutes but otherwise as competitors inside 'social science' faculties. 'Many economists are not sure whether they are social scientists or not, and more psychologists are included to think they are "life" scientists or possibly "human" scientists' (Cherns, 1979: 85).

Their principal interest lay in securing support for work that would bring disciplinary kudos (later, this came with a pound sign attached, as research assessment intensified), with the minimum of conditionality; they rejected themes and priorities (what the Council described as 'strategic' research) as dirigisme and illegitimate interference in the life of mind. This ran the risk of hypocrisy, as Albert Cherns pointed out (using the male pronoun). 'The social scientist cannot simultaneously claim support on the grounds of the usefulness of his work to the aims of government and arrogate to himself the choice of what work he will do' (Cherns, 1972: xix). But this was a battle they largely won, though they have rarely acknowledged the victory. The consequence has been that knowledge belonged to them.

The story of the Council wraps into the history of social science's impact; however percussive that noun, the tale cannot be reduced to disciplinary growth and the expansion of private knowledge and the ever greater array of titles of learned journals. Nor whether, over the years, the Council did manage to pull together the fissiparous tribes into a community. (The half-century verdict is doubtful.) At some point the 'social knowledge' produced under the aegis of the Council must touch on public, politicians and profit-makers and be judged in use. Among public concerns over the past 40 years, inflation falls dramatically as a worry into the early 1980s; unemployment rises then falls to a marginal anxiety. Trade unions disappear. The NHS rises during the later 1980s into the 1990s, along with schools. New worries appear – crime, migration and race, terrorism. Old worries – housing – fade. Should social science mirror these concerns in terms of the balance of investigation; did public spending through the Council reflect such public priorities? Should social science have educated opinion, on the basis of empirical study, data collection and consequentialist argument, including the opinion of policy makers who may be putting resources into issues – crime – that elicit public alarm but don't need spending, according to the 'evidence'? This short account is intermittently sceptical. That is partly because 'shaping' and influence logically require a degree of attention to communication, dissemination and public awareness, of which the record shows only sporadic signs.

A collector of opinion data is Ipsos Mori, along with TNS BRMB, YouGov and others. They are social science companies. Their business is data, methodology and prediction. Once, the ESRC could showcase the views of Gallup's managing director, Gordon Heald; he regretted not finding an 'academic home' for his firm's cross-national and longitudinal study of values and attitudes (Heald, 1990). Now research is strictly bifurcated. Commercial companies are underlabourers, providing the field force for sample surveys; they are not invited to sit at the top table as knowledge generators.

IMPRESARIO?

The intellectual health and development of the social sciences should be the concern of a strategist or impresario; would the role ever have been open to the Council? There have been hints at this wider oversight. For example in 1975 the SSRC supported an inquiry into learned societies which were struggling. Here might have been an opportunity to fashion a transcending social science identity above that of individual disciplines. But it was only several years later that the Association of Learned Societies in the Social Sciences was formed, a sickly child. Its progeny, the Academy of Social Sciences, struggles to make headway against the academic tides. The ESRC has supported the Strategic Forum for the Social Sciences and initiatives to coordinate data resources. But the forum lacks people from business as well as clout (British Academy, 2008). Strategy is easier to invoke than to deliver. A senior civil servant – Richard Bartholomew, head of research at the Department for Education – said 'we bring these things together by working alongside the academic community and the research councils to identify the areas of future data we need to pursue commonly' (Science and Technology Committee, 2012: 24). But that 'working' is at best informal and intermittent. Since the creation of the SSRC, UK government – the point has applied pretty much in the same way to the devolved administrations since 2000 – got on with its own versions of social (science) research in parallel and often indifferent to what the Council was doing. The state has a substantial internal social and economic research function, lets a large volume of research contracts and seeks varieties of evidence, some from universities, some from think tanks and intermediate bodies of varying intellectual pedigree. The division of labour between the Council and this function is unclear. For example, the coalition's data white paper said government social researchers would routinely 'archive research data' – a proposal undiscussed with the ESRC that would, had it been implemented, have cut across several existing initiatives (Cabinet Office, 2012).

So any picture of state knowledge that started or finished with the ESRC would be seriously deficient – leading to such knowledge was one of the reasons for creating the SSRC. Another puzzle to be described, if not solved.

HOW MUCH IS ENOUGH?

Maximum consensus gathers around the bland assertion that social science is worthwhile. Social science, that is, on a catholic definition as the study of people, their attitudes, culture, behaviour, market transactions, voting and so on. But favouring more human self-understanding gives no guide to how much (beyond a glib 'more') should be supported from public funds, nor does the general favourable proposition endorse this or that research application, journal article or finding. It may be (academics might say) that the Council's vocation was to advance social science knowledge, to which the only applicable evaluative criteria are immanent and internal to the club of disciplines. But even the club has difficulty with more and better/worse assessments.

Charles Lindblom uttered the base proposition. 'Most people believe that the answer (to making policies more effective) lies in bringing more information, thought, and analysis into the policy-making process' (Lindblom, 1980: 11). But social science knowledge is not immanent; it does not leap, like a salmon, from the racing waters of disciplinary debate into a pond where patient political and policy anglers sit with their rods. Knowledge for what is an old query: all answers are normative, i.e. to make things 'better'.

But what if, another analogy, knowledge is sequestered from birth in a dungeon and never sheds its light? The Council has paid for production but spent much less on communication and consumption (accepting those costive nouns don't capture what actually happens when people read, mark and fail to inwardly digest). The reason has to do with ownership. If knowledge belongs to the university or the discipline, it's they who should pay attention to the theory or practice of sharing and dissemination. But they don't. The doyenne of evidence-for-policy thinking, Carol Weiss, observed that what social scientists say – their theories, thinking, taxonomy – may shape the nature of the problems perceived by public and policymakers (cited in Wilson, 2002: 9). But a precondition for such enlightening influence is being there, being present in debate: it's communication; the other precondition is sympathy and sensitivity to public mood and policy makers' possibilities.

It would be possible to list all projects supported by the Council over the years and tie them to articles and books. But that, at best, would register only 'arrival' – the moment of academic publication. There are many more such moments. But if social science academics now publish in a greater number of journals than 50 years ago, is the resulting weight in and of itself valuable? 'Valuable' could be a functional (consequentialist) judgement along the lines: more knowledge has led to better decisions (assuming they can be independently measured). Or else 'valuable' is a normative statement, of a kind which, if made by a group less (allegedly) disinterested than academics, would be suspicious.

Still, some effort must be made to judge the 'enough' question. Enough resources, enough focus, enough impact? Did the Council concentrate 'enough' on public spending itself, or the components of GDP growth, or institutional reformation? The SSRC was born in a decade of public spending growth (by about 9 per cent of GDP over the 10 years from 1960), but also of worries about what later was called the supply side of the economy. In retrospect, modernisation efforts (the civil service, technical education) failed. Tax is an example of an arena of knowledge in deficit – it was acknowledged from the late 1960s that the tax authorities monopolised the field, crimping both policy making and analysis (Robinson and Sandford, 1983). That gap prompted Nils Taube, Dick Taverne and others to get the Institute for Fiscal Studies (IFS) going. Charles Sandford for a time ran the Centre for Fiscal Studies at the University of Bath. Why did it lapse, when the volume of tax research is insufficient? The IFS now scoops the pool. Why no concerted attempt to irrigate the fields of policy, practice and public understanding of taxation? Such examples of disjuncture – loose ends of knowledge – are everywhere.

But knowledge doesn't 'grow' if – the purpose but also the curse of social science – new knowledge undermines what went before. During the half-century, women 'arrived', as teachers and researchers and as critics and reformers of models and ways of thinking. Most of the social science that went before – and much since – was gendered in ways that reduced its claims to be about 'the business of people' and made it more like 'the business of men'. How should we evaluate the changed contours of knowledge as consciousness grew and in growing subverted and diminished what went before? It's not a matter of science but values. Ways of trying to know the world are deficient if they leave women out or are not done by women.

It's not just gender. Surely a machine for producing knowledge about economy and society bears some responsibility for the direction taken by actors in economy and society. Did it support work that should have informed them; if so, were they informed; did they behave as if they knew what the research and analysis said? Take the corporate sector. John Kay contrasts mission statements from a company such as ICI over our half-century:

> The one said, 'Our aim, our objective, is the responsible application of chemistry and related sciences. And through achieving that aim, we will make money for our shareholders, the community, etc.' And with that in mind, they moved from one business to the other gradually over a period of years and were Britain's leading industrial company. They then decided to focus on creating shareholder value and within a decade had lost most of the shareholder value with which they started. (Kay, 2015)

Shareholder value is a practice and instrument for enrichment of an interest group, but it is also an idea promulgated and discussed in public arenas, among politicians and regulators as well as in boardrooms. If we say such an idea is too far away from the elaborations and work of economists and students of business organisations (supported by the Council), we are making a candid admission about the relevance of their work. If we say shareholder value was advanced on the back of work supported by the Council, that would ascribe unwelcome responsibility for what – many would argue – has been a malign, even dysfunctional development in modern British capitalism. And if we say shareholder value advanced despite work done by the Council, that sounds like a confession of impotence and marginality.

In fact, it's well nigh impossible to say anything. We simply don't know enough about the genealogy of prevalent socio-economic ideas and perceptions. Examples tend to be asserted rather than demonstrated – for example the alleged dependence of Google on social network theory developed (in the US mostly) two decades ago. There is, putatively, some relationship between the production of knowledge by social scientists over the years and its use. But quite what it is, we can't say.

2
THE ESRC TODAY

SUMMARY

The ESRC is an arm's-length body, part of a notoriously disconnected Whitehall machine. During 2015 we learnt that its very existence remains contentious. UK social science lacks coherence and voice and the ESRC's responsibilities for it are limited, despite its role as supporter of postgraduate training and provider of data infrastructure. Its own place in the state's knowledge apparatus is uncertain: commissioning knowledge but not owning it.

When its 50th year began, the ESRC was sitting securely, apparently, in the thick of the state's knowledge production apparatus. That phrase is outlandish. Apparatus implies there is some joined-up mechanism; in fact there is no central oversight or even recognition of such a thing as 'state knowledge', including knowledge about economy and society. Critics often accuse the UK of centralism: Whitehall is overweening, they say. Yet Whitehall itself is a convenient fiction. Much of what the Council has done – which is to produce knowledge at second hand, through contracts with universities that aren't contracts in any enforceable or formal sense – is invisible to the rest of the centre, including the other cogs in the machine producing knowledge. Usually the 'centre of the centre' (the Treasury, Number Ten, the Cabinet Office) is indifferent. A parliamentary select committee might ask who has knowledge oversight. The answer is no one. The nearest approximation is a weak and obscure committee, albeit chaired by the permanent secretary of the Treasury, that notionally looks across the central state's knowledge and research activities – but the remit of the committee (comprising departmental heads of the analytical professions plus the chief executive of the Office of National Statistics – the ONS) does not cover the research councils, which belong to not 'the government' but a single parent department (Business Innovation and Skills, or BIS).

Perhaps this guarantees pluralism in the state's generation of knowledge; perhaps it's just a mess. Either way, great care must be taken – which is not always the case with conspiracy-minded social science academics – in talking about 'government' as a single entity. The Council might once have looked as if it should be central to the state's knowledge economy, but not now. Besides, there is no centre. The ESRC is one of seven semi-autonomous bodies that make up Research Councils UK (RCUK, founded 2002). Its 2015–16 budget is £2.6 billion, which makes up about half of the total public science and research; figures are not precise because of machinations involving what is defined as capital. The ESRC's budget is just under 6 per cent of the RCUK total (BIS 2014).

In typically British fashion, RCUK is not a statutory body and so is not open to queries about its lawfulness or formal accountability. It's an informal committee, more or less supervised by civil servants on behalf of ministers. It and they make up the rules as it goes along. It used to have a powerful director-general; the post was abolished; during 2015 it once again acquired a chief executive. Today the Government's Chief Science Adviser aspires to subject RCUK to more control. By autumn 2015 the RCUK was 'in play'; it's future uncertain. In December 2014, BIS announced a review by Sir Paul Nurse, president of the Royal Society. Again, it's a very British way of doing things. If the reviewer had complete discretion, his options ought logically to include self-immolation: he should be able to conclude there is no point in the review. Instead, he is enjoined to recommend change. The reasons behind a review seem to include the wish to integrate R&D spending with regional policy and rebalance economic growth, also realigning Whitehall science and research council spending. Just after the 2015 general election the new BIS secretary, the Thatcherite Sajid Javid, secretly set up another review of the research councils by the management consultants McKinsey. Were the two reviews by any chance related?

Collectively, so says BIS, the seven research councils 'provide public investment in science and research across the full spectrum of academic disciplines from the medical and biological sciences to astronomy, physics, chemistry and engineering, social sciences, economics, environmental sciences and the arts and humanities' (BIS, 2014). Note that separation of economics from the social sciences. Distinguishing 'economics' may be an accidental riff on the ESRC's title that stems from the attempted assassination of the organisation in the 1980s (see Chapter 3). Or it might deliberately reflect the civil service view that economics is not social science. There is a Government Economic Service separate from Government Social Research; its head of profession is big in the Treasury. Meanwhile, neither economics nor social research is 'science', for official purposes. Nurse would not have dreamt of including in science the provision of economics advice to government.

Situating the ESRC is at once straightforward and difficult. The UK state has no explicit policy for knowledge but does advertise a policy for research, led by RCUK. (The state knowingly spends on knowledge in health, defence and other domains so, inferentially, has fragments of a policy.) RCUK confronts 'societal challenges'. Those, also known as 'grand challenges', are Global Uncertainties; Digital Economy; Ageing; Living with Environmental Change; Energy; Global Food Security. By the sound of it, the ESRC and possibly the Arts and Humanities Research Council, the Benjamin of the RCUK, ought to be in the front line, but the STEM subjects – science, technology, engineering and maths – rule the roost and their respective research councils are higher in the pecking order.

The absence of an acknowledged policy for knowledge is a theme of this book, helping explain the ESRC's dislocated and marginal role. Streams of funding that support academic research are also not joined up. Universities do the bulk of RCUK research; they are charities; their governance is semi-private. Another arm's-length body, the Higher Education Funding Council for England together with its analogues for the devolved administrations, offers limited knowledge oversight, but its version of knowledge is disciplinary. The funding council looks to be a sacrifice on the bonfire of BIS quangos; administration of QR payments will be less 'bureaucratic'. The Research Excellence Framework 2014 demonstrates this. The REF is a scheme for (Quality-Related, or QR) payments to universities that qualify, running from 2016 to 2020 – they are worth £1.6 billion in 2015–16 (BIS 2014). Money is allocated to sectors (social science is one) and specific disciplines within them. The REF forbade, for example, work being submitted to different disciplinary panels, emphasising their autarky.

Some academics will take exception to the phrase above, 'policy for knowledge', saying it is an oxymoron. Knowledge is discovered; anticipation must fetter exploration. We will need to flesh out the contention later, in Chapter 5. Suffice it to say here that the very existence of a public body implies policy. Money is never going to be just shovelled out of the door. The relative position and support for individual disciplines constitutes 'policy'. Economics' dominance among the social sciences reflects not (necessarily) its intellectual strength but its ideological compatibility. It's arguable that the Council's functioning as a 'club' or 'mutual' protected those disciplines, sociology and politics especially, that would have been marginalised if signals from the political system had been more closely read and acted upon.

The restriction of research council support to academics implies it (on the state's behalf) believes in epistemological hierarchy, on top of which sits peer-reviewed, disciplinary knowledge: that, for practical purposes, constitutes 'truth' or, as the ESRC prefers, 'excellence'. Other knowledge is subordinate. But this organising principle is rarely articulated or its implications explored. Social science academics are generally progressive in their politics, if not overtly social democratic; as a matter of principle they dislike hierarchy and insinuations of superiority or elitism. Instead of asserting that what they do is primordial, they usually just ignore other producers of social knowledge, wrapping their forms of publication and restricted communications networks around them as blankets.

SITUATING THE ESRC IN THE CONSTITUTION – DEMOCRACY

As a public body, the ESRC makes an effort to reach out. Cautiously. The tabloids and their internet equivalents have not always been as indifferent to the alleged excesses of social research as they have been in recent years (Haslam and Bryman, 1994). Once, the ESRC press office spent its time fighting fires fuelled by stories about waste and banality. Research grants are still more or less subjected to the *Daily Mail* test – if they came to the attention of Paul Dacre would they end up in a prominent position in a right-wing tabloid newspaper as an example of waste or 'left-wing bias'? Investigation of the political and cultural power of the right-wing press has not been a strong pursuit by the ESRC.

Media markets are segmented. Knowledge and the appetite to know are stratified. In certain strata, social curiosity may be strong, which may explain the ESRC's successful launch of its annual 'Britain in ....' series. *Britain in 2012* sold 16,000 copies and could even be purchased at WH Smith. That is an achievement, but interpreting it is not easy. How is the ESRC's contribution to public enlightenment distinct from the work done by Ipsos Mori in pumping out polling and social data, or that of the ONS or government departments, with stories to tell about population, policies and places?

Despite Council efforts, social science does not enjoy much of a profile in parliaments and assemblies, which we can use as a proxy for democracy at large. A couple of months after the May 2015 general election the Institute of Government published a 'how to' guide for incoming members of House of Commons select committees, hoping to sharpen an often variable and unpredictable performance (Institute for Government, 2015). It makes no explicit mention of social science. MPs, Commons clerks, ministers and most witnesses inhabit a world where knowledge is intensely practical; it's about specifics and rooted in circumstance. Occasionally committees will fly, looking ahead at grand strategies. Knowledge from social science research is present in the mix but rarely labelled as such. For any given inquiry by MPs it's probably the case that knowledge from research could help, but a lot of digging and filtering and rendering are needed to present it in a useable form. Would extraction and refinement be worth the effort? Today's Westminster knowledge apparatus isn't capable, and no one else looks fit for such heavy lifting.

Theoretically – and much discussed over the years – some new cadre of intermediaries might step up. Simultaneously they would deal sympathetically with researchers and swim (comfortable alongside the flotsam and jetsam?) in the knowledge pool inhabited by the MPs and Commons staff – whose attention is necessarily short term and keyed to specific questions. Should such intermediation spring from *production* (practically speaking, research grant givers)? In our zero sum world, supporting consumption would have to be subtracted from resource available for research. Historically, academics have not been prepared to trade the pursuit of new or more knowledge against synthesis or spread of existing knowledge.

The ESRC confronts the problem inexplicitly. It hopes the researchers it supports will themselves reach out and share, but respects their autonomy too much to push and probe on whether they do – and certainly does not subject them to assessment of their performance as sharers/disseminators/co-producers. It runs events in parliament, to which MPs are invited, under the auspices of the All-Party Parliamentary Group on social science. It paid for the insertion of a social scientist into the Parliamentary Office for Science and Technology (http://www.parliament.uk/mps-lords-and-offices/offices/bicameral/post/fellowships/esrc/), which had not previously recognised social science. (This suggests the ESRC accepts systemic responsibilities for social science knowledge.) But knowledge and information at Westminster are fragmented. No strategy makes the respective roles of POST and the House of Commons Library and the Clerks' department coherent; MPs rely additionally on their own staff, who may include specialists, and infinite varieties of informal advice. In addition, analysis and data are supplied by the National Audit Office (NAO). Notionally owned by the legislature, the NAO occupies contested space between the executive (HM Treasury), the legislature, the wider public sector and, since the demise of the Audit Commission, local government. Research knowledge – and the ESRC – can only ever be tributaries into the pool, in which MPs may occasionally dip a toe. The liquid flows unpredictably, often a dribble, never in spate. There are no gauges, no weirs. And that makes the ESRC hard to classify.

SITUATING THE ESRC IN THE CONSTITUTION – QUANGO

The Council is a quango. It is co-eval with the Schools Council, which was abolished in 1982 and its functions scattered, illustrating the contingency of arm's-length status. ESRC staff are not civil servants, but their terms and conditions are geared to Whitehall's, and if the parent department, now Business Innovation and Skills (BIS), says administrative costs have to fall or back office services have to be shared with other bodies, it's command and control. When, in 2010, Cabinet Office minister Francis Maude declared a freeze on all 'marketing' by government, the ESRC had to submit even such innocuous events as its Festival of Social Sciences for inspection by his officials (personal communication).

But like other quangos, the research councils exercise discretion and are quite separate from other parts of the machine. The rubric says relations are productive and strategic: ad hoc and discontinuous describe them as well. On their governing boards (councils) academics predominate. It wouldn't do to exaggerate their cohesiveness. These days vice chancellors form a club separate from ordinary professors, eminent though they may be. But they all belong to a single university interest group. Their default is a generalised demand for more. Other members of boards/council ostensibly represent business, the public and voluntary sectors. Those who emphasise the identity of the ESRC as an organ of state might latch on to the presence at the council table of high representatives of Whitehall, including a senior official responsible for research and, in addition, the Treasury – during my tenure the government's chief economic adviser, Dave (now Sir David) Ramsden. The Treasury's interest in policy at large is usually small. Its officials want to deliver spending totals and are often indifferent to the detail of departmental life. Whitehall's view of social science is either hazy or outsourced to the Treasury which, given its identity as the economics department, is concerned with the fate of that one discipline, in terms of postgraduate flow, the quality of macroeconomic studies and the support of providers of data and analysis, including (despite its jagged criticism) the IFS.

What all this amounts to is a rebuttal of the argument academics sometimes make that the ESRC is intelligible as a transmission mechanism for imposing the will of the state on recalcitrant social scientists. This is no crankshaft and axle. When, after an election, ministers arrive at education or work and pensions, it's usually with a set of manifesto commitments that civil servants have studied in advance; the machine then delivers draft legislation or a switch in executive delivery. No one pitches up at Polaris House in Swindon with a sheet of A4 containing the Blair or Cameron formula for social science. The British central state is notorious for simultaneously displaying deep unity (in the culture, formation and preconceptions of permanent officials) and strong, even dysfunctional commitment to departmental and sectional interests. Governments are motivated by ideology but that rarely translates into a strategy, meaning a common template for their policy, conduct or administrative forms, as the Commons Public Administration Select Committee has often complained (PASC, 2012). During the Cameron era an ideological push to shrink the state, given cover by an alleged fiscal emergency demanding 'austerity' (Toynbee and Walker, 2015), was compatible with autarchic and even contradictory strands in departmental policy. The 'will of the state' may even take divergent tracks inside BIS.

The governance of social science is far from linear and certainly not to be summarised in a formula such as 'neo-liberal ministers ordain research to benefit UK plc or (capital accumulation through) private firms'. The biggest reason why such characterisation is wrong is that both the ESRC and social science are not – or at least not often – in the political line of sight. Social science is largely invisible in budget setting.

The theme is the ambiguity of arm's-length status, which is also observable in quangos in, say, the arts and broadcasting. For the ESRC, a BIS minister signs off appointments. Before that he or she may put an asterisk beside names on a list of candidates, indicating they really should be considered (without, the hovering civil servant will say, in any way injuring the autonomy of the process). That sounds conspiratorial. When the rewards at stake are so small – ESRC council members get a scant few thousand pounds – it's hardly nepotism for a minister to suggest a political ally, who also possesses experience and capacity. They rarely do.

Ministers may, however, get religion. The great example from recent times is the minister for science and higher education in the Cameron coalition, David Willetts. History may finger Willetts as the man responsible for a massive increase in the state's indebtedness through unrepaid student loans. It may also credit his personal support for social science research, including a mid-decade birth cohort study, securing upwards of £30 million from a largely indifferent Treasury.

For all his personal interest, Willetts was never minister for social science. That matters when government supports much social research outside 'science'. There is even a social science department of a kind in the form of the ONS, which analyses the data it collects. (Its governance is complex. The National Statistician is line-managed by the Cabinet Secretary; ONS is for most practical purposes under Treasury supervision. Its core revenue budget is slightly more than the ESRC's.) Since 1971 the statistical agency has even had its own journal, *Population Trends*; from the 1971 census it has conducted a longitudinal survey that still runs, alongside those the ESRC supports. Under figures such as John Boreham and Claus Moser the statistics and survey agencies broke new ground, analytically and methodologically.

Relations between the ONS and the ESRC are governed by no protocols or anything public. Conversations take place, at various levels, but not – in my experience – between the council and the ONS top board, which is now part of the UK Statistics Authority (UKSA), another arm's-length affair. The division of labour is opaque. The ESRC turned to the UKSA to invigilate its administrative data programme; the ONS is trying to build administrative data into the next census. Meanwhile ONS commissions academics, for example to work on how the national accounts should measure drugs and prostitution. This exercise did not produce a meeting of minds. The European Union told national statistical agencies to count illicit economic activity. Stephen Pudney and colleagues from the University of Essex responded that uncertainties in measuring illegal transactions made incorporating the new standard for drugs 'a mistake' (ISER, n.d.b.: 15).

Other departments and agencies also do social science, though it is rarely labelled as such. For example the Medical Research Council is custodian of various cohort studies. Longitudinal socio-economic-medical data is a jumble, which very few know about in its entirety – certainly not the government (MRC, 2014). Government departments, the devolved administrations and (to a small extent) local authorities conduct their own research and commission studies. There are at least 60 'public sector research establishments' (BIS, 2014b). Among them NHS bodies, the British Library and English Heritage are likely producers of social knowledge. We don't know for sure; the authors of the survey say their 'diverse character' makes it hard to know what to include, let alone what they do. There is no 'social science budget', not even an attempt to keep tabs on the different streams, let alone coordinate them. Connexions between these bits of government are informal and sporadic. In testimony to MPs (Science and Technology Committee, 2012: 16), ESRC officials spoke of working with the ONS and departments to ensure coherence, amid 'regular dialogue'. Who, then, is ultimately responsible for setting the parameters for what is required (of social science by government)?, asked the committee chair, Andrew Miller MP, at that same session. Good question.

SCIENCE POLICY

Social science is in but not of official science. The ESRC is well integrated into RCUK; the government's chief science adviser says the social sciences and humanities properly belong to the knowledge base; but public policy arguments about science remain stubbornly indifferent to the cost, value and function of social science-derived knowledge. The science budget is divvied up in obscurity – usually according to historic share. Ostensibly, the Nurse review

was set up because of discontent with such incrementalism (now, in austerity, its converse). But more rational division of the science cake implies both
the 'policy for knowledge' discussed earlier and much clearer recognition than
hitherto of the idiosyncratic nature of social science knowledge.

When the Cameron coalition appointed Nurse, discussants made much of
the danger to the Haldane principle (IUS Committee, 2009: para. 138ff.). At
its most banal, Haldane is no principle but rather a statement of administrative
functionality. Difficult (and often distributive) decisions are best devolved to a
specialist organisation working at arm's-length from ministers. What Haldane
had attempted, after the First World War, was a division of labour between
kinds of knowledge. Deeper and longer-term inquiries should be undertaken by
the arm's-length body; shorter run work of direct interest to ministers should be
commissioned directly by the government department. Over the years Haldane
had morphed into an assertion, at its most extreme, that public money for science be handed over to academics for them to spend on what interested them.
A weaker variant was that the political system might legitimately set both a
total and proffer guidelines about distribution between research councils under
the banner of national priorities, which you might trust elected politicians to
identify more readily than subject-fixated scientists.

In social science (invisible to Haldane and most science policy making
since) the division has never been clear cut. Governments are interested in
problems. They want business to make profits. The social science council con-
demns itself to irrelevance if it is not seen – or can simulate – contributions to
realising these goals. As for science at large, the funding argument is carried
on through a set of non sequiturs and on the basis of fuzzy empirical connection. The principal non sequitur is between UK academic excellence (defined
by citations) and national economic performance; in recent times they appear
to have an inverse relationship. The evidence linking 'science' spending and
the latter is of a general kind and focuses on one sector, manufacturing, which
has been diminishing in importance. Intuitively, social science understanding
should become more prized in a service-oriented economy; that has not been
reflected in the funding debate. ESRC interventions are sporadic and muted.

THE ESRC AS COMMISSIONER

Like all public bodies, including universities, the ESRC has been inflected by
the New Public Management and its rhetoric of targets, transformation and
perpetual innovation. But while local authorities, the NHS, other arm's-length
bodies and government departments are required to contract formally with

external suppliers, research councils do so informally and in ways that obscure rather than enforce accountability.

The ESRC engages in formal – auditable – transactions with universities over payment of sums for staff and IT. Yet the organisation's balance sheet and annual report make for odd reading. What gets purchased with ESRC money is not accounted for. Grants are paid gross: detailed breakdown of spending is not required. The council assumes the universities have their own accounting policies for travel and reimbursement of expenses. In NAO terms this is peculiar. Universities are not quizzed over their use of resources, for example what they pay their vice chancellors. Some universities behave as if they were commercial entities, borrowing on the strength of their balance sheets. But the research councils treat universities as part of a 'community', with moral characteristics. In social science, the question of ownership of results or intellectual property has not been given much attention, presumably because so few have had market value. Small print in the ESRC annual report tells us that – as a matter of course – the universities take ownership of the computers and equipment paid for by the ESRC. They also lay claim to data sets.

THE ESRC AND THE UNIVERSITIES

A striking aspect of the Council-university transaction is the ambiguous nature of the contract. It may specify duration of grant. It may demand that research reports are lodged with Swindon and data deposited with the UK Data Service. But once formalities are observed, research contracts make few substantive requirements. Few such contracts have risk registers and no attempt is made to predict, model or compensate for 'failure'. Researchers are deemed to have 'done the work' but are rarely held accountable for failing to validate the besetting proposition or establish an asserted causal relationship or – if the nature of the question demands it – produce a convincing account of why no answer was or could be forthcoming. Their 'failure' may indeed be welcome.

The ESRC interacts with universities at various levels – its staff visit deans and vice chancellors and it publishes various research protocols. In recent years these have focused on volume of grant applications, with the ESRC trying to massage it down in response to overall success rates as low as one in seven. (Success rates in social science have tended to be lower than elsewhere. For instance the MRC success rate in 2013–14 was one in four.) From 2011, the ESRC asked universities to screen applications before submission, allowing it to pay for a higher proportion of what it actually received. Since then, the ESRC has also raised the financial threshold for grants, refusing standard grant applications priced under £350,000. This connects with a complex conversation with specific disciplines and their varying rates of successful grant application (psychology, sociology and economics with success rates of 15, 8 and 10 per cent respectively in 2013–14) (ESRC, 2015c) and, usually below the radar, considerations of geographical and institutional balance and perceived fairness. In social science, as elsewhere in research funding, a fairly consistent pattern of concentration has held during the past decades, with very few successful applicants coming from outside a group of around 20 universities, on which perch a small number of top institutions, never officially recognised as such but immediately obvious from a cursory glance at receipts. They have large bargaining power. They reduce potential leverage by the Council on the research programmes and centres it establishes. Yet their power is rarely discussed in the open, or their impact on social science research policy.

In recent times, receipts (especially research income) have become a tool of performance management in universities, some of which now impose targets on departments and individuals. How this scheme for managing necessarily limited grants connects with wider considerations – the utility of the research, especially – is not at all clear. Martyn Hammersley, emeritus professor of educational and social research at the Open University, complains that grant income has come to matter more than 'the value of the research proposed or how well it is carried out' (Hammersley, 2015). But as we have seen, his conception of value is itself internal to the academic system. It seems to be based on a utopian idea of unlimited funding for all research deemed interesting by the interested parties, the academics. In Hammersley's view any rate less than 100 per cent is injurious to the advancement of knowledge, which should be illimitable.

THE ESRC AND THE SOCIAL SCIENCE SYSTEM

The ESRC talks to the universities, yes, but it is not responsible for social science within them. By its own lights, the ESRC is the primary UK funder of long-term strategic social science research. It 'coordinates the national social science research capacity and capability to address [societal] challenges and delivers a continuous supply of skilled people and appropriate research infrastructure to address them in the future' (BIS, 2014a).

The social science ecology is fed by choices made at A-level, determining the flow of undergraduates, which in turn stocks postgraduate numbers and the supply of staff to employers. Interconnections are usually random; the ESRC does not have the reach to be (its self-ascription) a national coordinator of capacity. Other public bodies and firms 'do' social science. They forecast (model) behaviour; they collect and analyse data about markets, the sensibilities of ethnic groups, the needs and purchasing power of social groups. They categorise and analyse the data they collect according to theories – which may or may not derive from work done contemporaneously or in the past by academics. Council programmes, such as that in the late 1990s on violence, may have touched deep levels of awareness – particularly about gender (Stanko, 2006). But as its director says, the 'impact' of (non-academic, value-committed) activism is easier to delineate than the flow of knowledge.

Company boards advance causal propositions about price and profitability. The DWP models behaviour and predicts the choices made by benefit recipients. Such work is un-self-knowing. If companies employ engineers or maintain laboratories, they usually are reckoned to be doing 'science' (or technology), which notionally falls under the gaze of an establishment headed by the Royal Society and the Royal Academy of Engineering. By contrast, social science can barely be said to exist as a sector. Companies employ economists, consultancies undertake research, firms grapple with marketing (influencing people's behaviour) and organisational function – but they don't think they are doing social science. Within the domain learned societies and subject associations exist and may even, in some areas, affect what firms do – by invigilating professional standards (for example in town and country planning and parts of data collection and statistics). But social science self-consciousness is missing. Ditto enforcement of standards. Companies, public relations chancers, charities and public authorities can mount what they call surveys, but many fail the most basic tests of method and reliability. Faltering attempts are made to identify and excoriate 'bad social science', by commentators such as Ben Goldacre and the truth and accuracy charity Fullfact, but their influence and effect are limited.

Somewhere in the sector are the independent research organisations. They were 'not tidy, predictable or easily comprehensible' in the 1970s (Cherns, 1979: 32); now, with the rise of the think tanks, the landscape is even more variegated. The National Foundation for Educational Research, Overseas Development Institute, the National Institute for Economic and Social Research (NIESR) and the Royal Institute of International Affairs are all contributors to the knowledge pool along with, less robustly, the politically-aligned think tanks. New organisations, such as the Resolution Foundation and the Education Endowment Foundation, do work of the highest standards. Elsewhere in the undergrowth of knowledge are RUSI (the Royal United Services Institute), consultants – notably McKinsey – and hybrids such as the Pensions Institute, located in a university business school.

It's a sector the ESRC makes no claim to lead. Since there are no alternative candidates, that means no leadership. The British Academy and the Academy of Social Sciences coexist with and depend on disciplinary associations and societies. They confer recognition, validate peer review and enforce epistemological discipline – on which, in turn, the research council depends. Social science has, over the years, struggled to 'make the case', hampered by internal disunity, enervating self-doubt and public and political reluctance to recognise what social scientists do as 'science', as opposed to accumulate expertise and knowledge. The Council has looked on, dismayed and powerless. 'One of the achievements of the SSRC has been to bring about a community of social scientists', observed Albert Cherns (1979: 39). It's not tightly knit.

SOCIAL SCIENCE CAPACITY

Unsung and largely out of sight, the Council has for 50 years paid for the supply of postgraduates – so guaranteeing social science has a future – and for 'infrastructure'. We will pick up in the next chapter how it took over a decade for the nascent SSRC to provide postgraduate support that consisted in more than throwing money at individuals and departments and letting them get on with it – or not, as was often the case. Since then, the Council has tried to insist that postgraduates are actually trained, rather than being abandoned to trial by PhD ordeal. Against academic opposition, the ESRC in 2010 established a national network of 21 Doctoral Training Centres. At best, they inject rigour into postgraduate training and might mitigate disciplinary autarky by encouraging a wider pan-social science perspective.

As early as 1967, the SSRC began to organise the basic material of social science inquiry – the results of surveys. It created an archive, which is now the UK Data Service, a giant compendium, including deposits by the ONS and others. But the ESRC struggles to ensure the data is exploited. Pick-up is haphazard, depending on chance inquiries, at the whim of individuals and – sine qua non – the capacity of researchers to handle data. Similar asymmetry is visible with the big longitudinal studies, the 1970 and Millennium cohorts and the British Household Panel Survey, expanded since 2008 into 'Understanding Society'. Value inheres not in the successive interviews with households or subjects on their life course but in interpretation, framing and interrogation – work for which the data gatherers may not themselves be fit. Infrastructure, then, points to ancillary and parallel policies for using data and ensuring there does exist a population of researchers able to use data. Standing in the way is the doctrine of academic autonomy and universities. The ESRC wants to make best use of the data it buys, but the only tools it seems to have are bribes (extra or new grants) such as the secondary data analysis initiative. But money can only be spent on people who are capable. Within a couple of years of the SSRC's birth, a deficit in quantitative skills among UK social scientists had been recognised – but has not since been remedied (British Academy, 2015). During the past few years, a new effort has been made to push methodological training and statistics among social science postgraduates, assisted by the ESRC, but the obstacles – dislike of numbers, inability to handle them, disciplinary inertia, even resistance – have so far proved hard to dislodge.

STRATEGIC AND EXCELLENT?

The ESRC differentiates *its* knowledge; it is deemed *strategic*. This could mean longer lasting – a question that deserves discussion (see Chapter 7). Strategy takes the form of responses to the set of 'challenges' distilled by RCUK from the ether of policy and public conversation. The implication is that strategic goes deeper than, say, answering a question for HMRC about taxpayers' likely behaviour or analysis of public sentiment by a firm such as Ipsos Mori. But also emblazoned on the Council masthead is 'excellence with impact'. This is another puzzle – is it an aspiration or an empirically demonstrated association along the lines of: the higher the intellectual quality of work, the more likely it is to be taken up by decision makers in organisations or government? The ESRC, like the higher education funding councils that followed it in emphasising the real world effect – impact – of academic knowledge, has not chosen to confront the possibility that the relationship between impact and academic excellence might be inverse or stochastic. Policy makers may be more stimulated by 'quick and dirty' than by long-run and academically respectable. The truth is that we simply don't know enough about policy outcomes to be able to make the call.

That leaves us in difficulty in pinning down the characteristics of the knowledge the Council exists to support. An example: In spring 2013 the ESRC supported the Association of Convenience Stores in convening the first Global Summit on Innovation in the Convenience Sector. The event brought together retailers, academics and suppliers from around the world: it 'provided a fantastic opportunity to promote social science and the ESRC' (ESRC, 2013c). This sounds plausible, but it might also have prompted the attendant managers of Londis and Express groceries to think the ESRC was in the business of helping them make ends meet and cope with volatile demand – work they might, if they had the money, turn to consultants to do. Similarly, with the 'knowledge navigator' the ESRC appointed for the retail sector. An obvious rejoinder would be: can you tell us how to succeed? The sharp question is whether 'strategic' knowledge can ever be made available to 'users' or whether it exists at a level of generality or abstraction that renders it, literally, useless (except for the purposes of academic conversation).

The ESRC evidently does a lot more than what is 'strategic'. It paid to survey 300 exotic dancers, one product of which was an iPhone app and website offering them information, for example, about staying safe (University of Leeds, 2012). It sounds useful but oddly random: why exotic dancers and not any wider group of sex workers? And were the 'changes to policy on licensing lap dancing' – claimed by the ESRC – more the result of a particular group of researchers intervening rather than a logical product of the research? It's not that 'excellent' social science cannot be done on dancers or corner shops; it's that the knowledge *people* can put to use ('impact') is different from what passes muster according to the (academic) criteria defining what is rigorous social science.

Impact is now an official criterion for distributing research money to universities through the Quality-Related channel. For its part the ESRC asks grant receivers to lay out their 'pathways' to impact and report after the fact. As academics have colonised impact – motivated by money – it has become the subject of papers in journals and earnest discussion, typically among academics rather than between them and those likely to be 'impacted'. For someone in business any principal impact is going to be measured in money. When the ESRC talks about improvements in the performance of small enterprises engaged in learning and networking programmes, the proof of the pudding is going to be whether those businesses made profits, survived or, as start-ups, allowed their owners to cash in quick. The ESRC wants businesses to benefit from interaction with academics but rarely specifies the difference between the knowledge it pays for and what business might acquire, as it were, off the shelf, from consultants or advisers. Again, likely measures are obvious. Did the proffered interaction with academics increase profit, turnover and employment? If that is too direct a question, we are left wanting something more cogent than participants' vague sense that knowledge is available (if indeed it is).

THE ESRC UNDER THE TORIES

The Council could and does itself decide what kind of knowledge it will pay for. It strives to discern 'national challenges' that exist outside or, as it were, beneath the contestation of parties and politicians. But that relocates the matter of accountability. Research funding must, in some way, reflect political (democratic) priorities. And they change, as in 2010 and 2015. So must knowledge necessarily reflect the concerns and interests of incumbents, here the Tory-dominated coalition?

The question implies the Tories have a settled view of what knowledge the state needs under their control. They don't; for example, the Nurse review was convened with no reference to the social sciences. If there were a straight read-across from governing ideology to ESRC budgets, it seems that right-wing governments like social science, even in austerity. The 2010–15 science budget was 'protected', relative to other parts of public spending. This 'flat cash' settlement was worth £153 million to the ESRC in 2015–16, down from £158 million in 2010; resources at its disposal were larger once capital allocations and joint ventures with government departments, such as international development, are included (BIS, 2010). In 2013 and again in 2014, planned allocations to the ESRC were scrapped, only for large slugs of money to be poured in, on condition they were spent with great haste and everyone involved signed up to define it as capital investment.

When chancellors get anxious about demand and growth – even when deficiencies in both are self-inflicted by erroneous macroeconomic policy – they find money quickly. Capital spending has cosmetic value. The ESRC got lucky in the lottery and, at short notice, was able to cobble together programmes, presentable as strategic (Big Data) investment. A case can be made that longitudinal data sets have some of the characteristics of 'capital investment'; they continue to add value over time (provided researchers ask the right questions). At speed, the ESRC convened a programme on administrative data. Partisans of the view that the ESRC is merely an agent of the state no doubt would cite this as an example of its pursuit of political interest – the Tories saw the exploitation of administrative data as a way of cutting costs and providing opportunities for outsourcing. Actually, the programme served to display the typical lack of coordination in British central government. The ESRC approach connected only haphazardly with that taken by the Medical Research Council and only intermittently with the various agencies concerned with personal data in the NHS, the ONS and the Cabinet Office, which had its own programme pushing more collaboration in using data generated in public interactions with the state to cut costs and smooth transactions. But the Cabinet Office minister Francis Maude was ineffective in selling the policy to his cabinet colleagues in, for example, the Treasury (parent of HM Revenue & Customs) or the Department of Work and Pensions, let alone health. Enthusiasm was lacking. The ESRC's involvement went largely unremarked.

As much by osmosis as any formal procedure, ESRC staff and BIS civil servants absorb a sense of the knowledge priorities of the government of the day. But even ideologically robust ministers operate in departments and silos; inter-visibility is often low; they may not notice research conducted in their own department that may have a distinctly social democratic and interventionist tinge. For example, the ESRC picked out from longitudinal studies a finding linking the length of time a mother breastfeeds and benefits for the child (Evidence Briefing, n.d.). The ESRC gloss, that policy should therefore focus on breastfeeding support in hospitals followed by longer-run intervention, seems to conflict with hairshirt austerity and spending cuts.

The ESRC's acceptability to ministers was tested in the 'Future of the UK and Scotland' programme. As the independence referendum approached, the ESRC could have sat on its hands. Instead, it boldly asserted that social science could enrich and enlighten debate before the vote in September 2014. Protagonists of the 'lackeys of the neo-liberal state' view should find this hard to parse. Whose interests was the ESRC sustaining by appointing Professor Charlie Jeffrey of the University of Edinburgh as coordinator of projects mostly run by academics in Scottish universities? Theirs, certainly, but not obviously those of the Scottish nationalists or the UK state. Civil servants in London approved the programme in principle in advance, with the caveat that they would like prior warning of 'findings' likely to excite controversy. Perhaps Treasury officials took it for granted that if the programme contained empirical studies of the finances of a separate Scottish state, they would demonstrate its unsustainability and implicitly endorse the union state. This proved correct – especially over the currency an independent Scotland would use.

But it was equally likely that academics in Scottish universities might be critical of the union state and lend their weight, implicitly, to separatism, which also happened. As a programme of research it was a mixed bag. In some cases existing ESRC centres responded in desultory fashion, hoping for money to allow them to go on doing what they were doing before. The rapid rise of Scottish nationalist sentiment and, in the 2015 general election, voting proclivity took the academic researchers as much by surprise as everyone else. But ministers (in Edinburgh as in London) implicitly bought a model of research as pure enlightenment: disinterested researchers would lay uninflected knowledge before (perspicacious?) voters whose decisions would be enriched and made more rational. This may even have happened. It's hard to know, since public enlightenment demands more and more sophisticated metrics than hits on a website or attendees at an Edinburgh seminar.

Assessing the ESRC under the Tories must include the way it anticipated ministers – research as a policy prophylactic. An obvious case is austerity itself, and whether the Council adopted or was forced into a role as intelligence gatherer for spending cuts. The opportunity existed. Effective spending depends on rigorous evaluation of policy implementation. The NAO was underwhelmed by civil service efforts, finding only patchy examples, even in presentations to the Treasury by departments during the 2010 spending review (NAO, 2013). The ESRC picked up the gauntlet.

Among senior Tory ministers was Oliver Letwin, who has had a curiously rich relationship with social science research. Letwin has a PhD in political philosophy. His parents were social science academics – albeit of a dissenting right-wing kind. Dissenting may not be quite the right word. Shirley Letwin was representative of the distinctly right-wing strand in LSE social science, surfacing in political science (Kenneth Minogue), economics (Lionel Robbins onwards) and sociology (Donald Macrae). Young Letwin had been special adviser to Sir Keith Joseph and shared his suspicion of social research. As Cabinet Office minister in the Cameron coalition, however, Letwin lent his weight to the creation of the 'What Works' network, intended to exemplify disinterested social science research.

Understanding 'what works' was always secondary to Letwin's attested aim of shrinking the state – he had been hidden away during the 2001 election for blurting out the ambition of reducing government to less than 35 per cent of GDP (http://news.bbc.co.uk/news/vote2001/hi/english/newsid_1334000/1334380.stm), an ambition now in sight, if Osborne's spending plans to 2020 are enacted. You can extract from his previous writings some backing for the idea that 'not working' is potentially a means of reaching the goal of cutting government back. His colleague Nick Boles expressed it pithily: 'chaos' was a way of softening up public services (*Guardian*, 2010).

WHAT WORKS

The Council has long been poised, uncomfortably, between supporting 'policy science' and backing the interests of academics, which might sometimes include policy evaluation (an activity otherwise within the province of government and non-academic organisations, such as the National Foundation for Educational Research). What Works is the latest occasion when ambiguity has been on display. What Works poses two kinds of issue. One is whether there can be neutral or technical policy analysis – evaluation that ignores the ideological and partisan bases of policy and assumptions about public spending and action. The second is how to align denser, more practical work with the 'strategic' and 'transformative' rubrics the research council had claimed for itself.

An odd tentativeness has characterised the programme, however. Muscular recommendations that the ESRC embroil itself in trials and direct participation in evaluation (for example from Shepherd, 2014) have been rejected in favour of a more distanced connexion, sort of payment without presence. So the ESRC supports, but does not run the centres. Some are conventional academic units, focusing on a particular question, for example the LSE's on urban and locational policies; this picks up similar work of long standing. Here, the Department of Communities and Local Government is a 'partner'.

Others, such as the crime and policing centre, are integral parts of the government's apparatus, with limited academic involvement (which may allow it to make recommendations on policing that justify the Tory policy of cutting police numbers). Yet others are social science in action, paralleling what academics have or have not done, for example the Early Intervention Foundation. They are linked in a network convened by David Halpern on behalf of the Cabinet Office. (Halpern, a former academic social scientist, is an intriguing interstitial figure, who moved from being a Blair special adviser to head the quasi-privatisation of the 'Nudge Unit', now the Behavioural Insights Team.)

Similar shadow surrounds recent (renewed) effort by the ESRC on small and medium enterprise. Although small business had been a focus of the Labour government, Tory affinities with the sector are strong. Some might judge the establishment of an Enterprise Research Centre (in January 2013) to show awareness of ministerial interests. Or those of the finance sector, given the centre is backed by the British Bankers Association to the tune of £800,000 (http://www.enterpriseresearch.ac.uk/about/sponsors/). Or it is simply in the national interest that the ESRC 'will increase collaboration with business, in particular across our priority areas for private sector engagement – retail, financial services and the green economy ... delivering research to support growth is a thread running throughout. ... We will support growth by improving our understanding of how business identifies and takes advantage of new market opportunities' (ESRC, 2015a). Is that 'our' generic or firm specific? Is the centre intended to assist small and medium-sized firms deal with balance sheet problems or provide distanced analysis at a level of abstraction far from the shop counter? What's unclear is how close research could or should get to daily practice, exemplified by a company's profitability. 'It may be true that wealthy people are more likely to become entrepreneurs, but the evidence is clear that entrepreneurship itself drives personal and household wealth' (ESRC, 2014b: 4). Social science makes you better off.

It would be extravagant to say the Cameron governments have had any policy for knowledge, but they have policies for data. The ESRC has been a player. It has mounted Big Data programmes, some seeking to bring social science academics into closer connection with companies (Tesco, Google) which extract commercial value from analysing data about their customers. It created the Administrative Data Service and associated research network, to promote the use of data from citizens' interaction with the state as an adjunct to, perhaps even a replacement for, data from surveys – for example, using tax records to follow the life course of young people previously enrolled in a cohort study.

The ESRC strategic plan is therefore hard to read (ESRC, 2015a). It is neither a set of inferences from ministers' likely interests nor is it innocent of rhetoric echoing what they might say (or what civil servants might write for them to say). Perhaps it's best described as an ideal type: what a 'small l' liberal, progressive and high-minded government might set out, in the belief that social science is positively useful focused on questions that 'most reasonable people' would identify as current, at a certain high level of abstraction plus a knowing acknowledgement of business interests. The knowledge being proffered (or at least promised) is to help understand socio-economic conditions and promote wellbeing 'for all', while reminding us of the harm resulting from 'excessive inequalities' and the broadly social or societal causes and consequences of climate change.

3

PROMISE AND DISAPPOINTMENT

SUMMARY

The bright hopes of the mid-1960s quickly gave way to disappointment, the research council a victim both of academic refusal or inability to supply requisite knowledge (as sought, for example, by Sir Keith Joseph) and the cultural and ideological turn against the social democratic state the SSRC symbolised. The story here is about marginalisation – in Whitehall – then the attempted assassination of the research council by the Thatcher government.

A child of its time, the SSRC photographed council members at their first meeting on 21 January 1966. As well as the heavy glass ashtrays on the table in front of them, the picture shows only two women, one of them a secretary, and the rest all white men (Nicol, 2001: 73). Council meetings now take place in smoke-free rooms, and the appointment of Jane Elliott as chief executive in 2014 was a marker of the social change the research council has existed to register and explicate. But there lies a problem of evaluation. Did it, as the founders envisaged, anticipate change and alert society, or were the social scientists it supported as surprised by reality and as empiricist in response as the rest of us?

The Council's half-century could be brightly narrated as a story of growth, interrupted by the slight abolition unpleasantness in the early 1980s, before movement to the sunny uplands of acceptance during the 1990s as a fully-fledged research council, supporting the production of knowledge in all forms, both fundamental and more immediately practicable.

A better reading reports initial (positive and positivistic) promise: more and deeper social knowledge as an instrument of general enlightenment and, especially, more effective and higher quality public policy. The SSRC was born at the same time as, for example, Neddy, the National Economic Development Council, amid faith that, supplied with knowledge, forecasts and data, managers would lift their game (PEP, 1966). The Government Economic Service was formally established in 1964, even though economists had been in the service of the state for years. This was '60s corporatism, when we would all pull together and knowledge would emancipate firms, unions, and government from the stagnation of the '50s. This reading would then note disappointment, even before the 1960s were out, with the collapse of modernism as a political and institutional faith. The Council was never in command of its own history; such is the fate of a subordinate quango. The story here is of the SSRC's marginalisation, ideological rupture and disloca-tion within social science disciplines. By the early 1970s the die was cast. There would be perpetual tension between government's self-assessed need for knowledge (expressed as themes or strategic priorities) and the capacity and willingness of academic social scientists to supply it, with the research council running to and fro between them. Government departments had already taken action. They would do their own social and economic research, leaving the research council in limbo. In this history ambiguity abounds: over the division of labour in knowledge production, between different streams of support for universities, over the volume and quality of knowledge needed by society and economy and, still, over the need for a social science research council. How far are things now settled – as, during 2015, the very existence of a separate research council for the social sciences has once again become a question crossing ministers' desks?

Party poopers at the 50th birthday ask whether the creation of the SSRC was a moment of hubris from which later rebounded the anti-statism and anti-progressivism that captured the intellectual high ground – and public policy – from the later 1970s onwards, and may still rule the roost. There's certainly evidence of a backlash against planning (O'Hara, 2007). Put that another way. Was the SSRC, as constituted in 1965, a wrong turn in the wider movement of knowledge production and dissemination? 'Wrong' is meaningless, unless we have a different, preferred trajectory. That might be to do with more effectively mobilising knowledge for practice. What if, during the late 1950s, the Human Sciences Committee of the Department of Scientific and Industrial Research had become the agency for social science, tying it more closely to markets, produc-tion and the economy? Or what if Whitehall had not responded to Heyworth by falling back on the proven administrative model of a 'science council'? Albert Cherns, who was there at the birth, says 'there is no self-evident reason why social science should not be part of social policy' (Cherns, 1979: 42). Say the Treasury had succeeded in its argument that the British Academy should dis-pense grants for social science as it did for history and archaeology. Say, long ago, the 'university monopoly' on research had been broken and freestanding institutions expanded, as had been proposed to the Clapham Committee (Nicol, 2001: 23). Say the Robbins Committee recommendations had been synchronised with Whitehall deliberations about research and debate about the expansion of higher education had paused to consider disciplinary trajectory and capacity.

ORIGINS AND DESTINATIONS

In retrospect, the creation of some kind of organising body for social science feels inevitable – a matter of when, not if. War had sharpened the state's awareness of gaps. In the late 1930s and during the Second World War, the political and administrative classes came together with academic leaders to agree that government needed to know more, to organise itself better, to fight and defend, to organise society, to promote markets and economic growth. Postwar, it needed data and analysis on 'problems' – real and imagined, including delinquency, single motherhood, industrial relations, migration, television, schooling. The Tories, in power from 1951, puzzled over how to accommodate social change in a prosperous society they prided themselves on furthering (Jarvis, 2005); social science might have ingratiated itself better with the right if it had made that problematic its own.

More knowledge implied dedicated and serious inquiry, i.e. research. Existing provision was fragmented, puny. Whitehall was suddenly aware of its inability to find out – for example the Ministry of Housing and Local Government in relation to housing and the Rent Act 1957. No academics were interested. Yet after the Rent Act came the Notting Hill Riots, the trial of Lady Chatterley, the Beatles and the Robbins Report: whatever this social thing was, government needed more. Consensus spanned the parties. But what was wanted was instrumental knowledge. The 'for what' question answered itself: for the sake of society, government and growth. Knowledge for the state, moreover: the prevalent belief was both that intervention was benign and that the producers of social knowledge were its toolsmiths. Social research and social improvement have had a long and passionate affair; state social research and state intervention ditto.

Neither the Clapham Committee (1946) nor, 20 years later, the inquiry led by Lord Heyworth (1965) thought in any great detail about what an arm's-length research body – rejected by one and accepted by the other – would actually do. The committee set up in 1945 under Sir John Clapham accepted the need for more research but – nobbled by academics, who preferred an increase in the university grant – it pronounced a research council premature, fearing 'premature crystallisation of spurious orthodoxies' (a great phrase that it's very hard to make sense of). The committees' witnesses from government and business were only semi-conscious of their own parallel role as producers of knowledge; they were not required to think about how it would mesh or compete. Whitehall departments were and remained ambiguous. By the 1960s they felt the research they commissioned was not enough: they wanted (someone) to do more 'fundamental' studies. This suggested a division of labour, the SSRC identifying the socio-economic problems requiring 'fundamental research' before civil servants spotted them. This 'strategic research', said Andrew Shonfield, was analogous to what a firm operating in oligopolistic market conditions might undertake, compared with a perfectly competitive firm: the rates of discount they applied to the future were inverse (Shonfield, 1972b). Shonfield's successors have held to the phrase. The problem for them, as for Shonfield, was willingness and capacity on the part of academic social scientists to think 'fundamentally' both outside the confines of their discipline and in terms that made – or would come to make – sense to decision makers in firms and government.

How far should a new agency be proactive, attempt to forecast, discerning shallows and dry areas in the pool of knowledge, then seeking to moisten them? Heyworth's map was limited to existing terrain. No one asked about areas fenced off, such as the Treasury's attempt to monopolise macroeconomics or socio-economic knowledge sequestered from public (or academic) inspection by enduringly powerful private interests, notably the banks – including (after its nationalisation in 1945) the ostensibly publicly-owned Bank of England. But even if knowledge could be coherently divided along an axis between 'strategic research' and what government needed to know day to day, a precondition was a 'close working relationship with government agencies by social scientists'. Shonfield's idea of social scientists being present to run experiments as policies change was never going to be realised.

EARLY YEARS

The SSRC was born when the expansion of higher education was in full spate yet no one scoped the likely relationship between public social science and universities, let alone what the institutional bases of 'strategic research' should be. The result, almost at once, was the multiversity – a problematic mix of teaching and research, never mitigating the pull of the disciplines towards abstraction and private knowledge, away from the public sphere. The question pending from the Clapham review was whether universities must be the sole suppliers of research knowledge; ought the SSRC to open up alternative, competing sources of research and analysis? Social scientists – possessors of the knowledge deemed by the decade's guiding spirits to be most useful – were in short supply. A major task of any new body would be training more. But only for universities? As for supplying knowledge, at first the SSRC was merely responsive, as if it were hoping questers would come to it with projects that answered its call. But Heyworth had said the worth of the Council would lie in its capacity to identify shortages, areas needing investigation. During the Young and Shonfield eras, the SSRC tried to 'think' for itself, even daring to establish its own research units – in the belief that the form and culture of dedicated and 'owned' research organisations might produce better research. Robin Matthews, Shonfield's successor, later reflected that 'how to give continuity to distinguished groups remains an unsolved problem' (Matthews, 1990). It still is. In the late 1960s, for the first and last time, the Council organised a set of subject reviews, on firms, consumer behaviour, poverty, automation and so on, 'to help keep abreast over a wider field … also providing those in industry, government, the educational world and elsewhere with information about recent developments' (Mitchell, 1968).

In retrospect, in that decade of modernisation and institutional rejigging, so much might have been sorted out. The Fulton Report proposed departmental planning units to which analysts trained in the social sciences would contribute (Fulton, 1968). The Cabinet Office created coordinating committees for social research. The former were never strong or mainstream; the latter faded and died. Permanent secretaries, few educated in the social sciences and few sufficiently intellectually curious to want to assay the knowledge needed for public policy, were programmed to fend off an organisation that purported to supply policy science. Perhaps it was inevitable that Whitehall would confront the SSRC just as it dealt with Fulton, and his proposals for making public service more expert. Typically the permanent secretaries appeared to play ball, for example collaborating with the SSRC in setting up Academic Liaison Officers (ALO). Young had high hopes: they would pull threads together, visiting universities and research institutes.

> A well publicised ALO system which fulfilled the functions proposed for it would have gone some way towards overcoming the difficulties caused by the exclusion of SSRC and foundation-supported research from the government machine and the consequent lack of interest by any part of that machine in the results of the research which the outside sponsors support. (Thomas, 1985: 45)

Those hopes withered away.

Departments, responding to activist ministers both before and after Ted Heath replaced Harold Wilson in 1970, were themselves doing research, among them the Civil Service Department (a post-Fulton creation, intended to modernise HR and staff management in Whitehall). In the 1970s, the giant Department of Health and Social Security became a major sponsor of social research, along with the Department of Education and Science (with Margaret Thatcher at its head).

Research profiles varied. Whitehall had no strategy for knowledge and wished to have none. The DES, the SSRC's parent, was the only ministry to have a strategy embracing its various knowledge bodies, which included the Schools Council. Permanent secretaries did not put knowledge high on their agendas; chief scientists had, again, hugely variable profiles. Political colouring was not necessarily what determined volume – the Department of Environment increased research during the 1980s, as did the Department of Employment. Under the latter, the Manpower Services Commission deployed knowledge ... to deal with matters of current concern, notably the school to work transition and youth unemployment. Exciting social science was commissioned by government. Halsey's educational priority areas, which the SSRC supported, had been anticipated by the community development projects launched when James Callaghan was Home Secretary – a rich mix of action research, contemporaneous evaluation and normative commitments.

Why didn't ministers – apart from Tony Crosland and Shirley Williams at education – pay more attention, especially those such as Dick Crossman and Wilson himself? You could write the history of the SSRC/ESRC without mentioning ministers, with the exception of Crosland, Keith Joseph, David Blunkett or, latterly, Willetts. Ministers, left or right, rarely do institutional detail nor strategy, and certainly never address such big, abstract questions as 'what does government need to know?'. So the administrative history of the research council followed a pattern seen in other arm's-length bodies. Much depended on chairs' nous and networks and, specifically, their access to ministers responsible for funding (and appointments). In its first decade, the SSRC established itself functionally, survived the change of government in 1970, and failed sufficiently to provoke the incoming Education Secretary (Margaret Thatcher). With Labour back in power in 1974, 'foundational' questions about the organisation's purpose forced themselves to the surface again.

THE PICTURE BY 1975

Growth was vertiginous. The number of postgraduates in sociology (including social administration) increased from under 1000 in 1965 to 2500 in 1975

(Bulmer, 1978: 29). But as precipitous was the growth in directly commissioned government research, which doubled in value in the three years after 1969 (Perry, 1976). In addition to central government the new large local authorities organised social science research teams. (Not all survived the decade; the Thatcher government abolished the Greater London Council and the metropolitan counties, which had been nodes of local social science work.) After the flush of '60s enthusiasm faded, the SSRC did not so much abandon the 'problem' focus of its birth as move to try to address it indirectly. The SSRC became a facilitator of academic research. It could try to prompt, suggest and dangle carrots; but conditions of supply and demand allowed the universities to entrench the doctrine of academic autonomy, which persisted and perhaps even strengthened even after market conditions for academic social science deteriorated in the 1980s. Left pretty much to itself – while following existing guidelines for organisation – management costs grew over its first decade and, in the absence of scrutiny, inefficiencies crept in. One of the most obvious (by the later 1970s) was the completion rate for PhDs, which fell to no more than a third.

The SSRC's first decade was a bright time for (public) social knowledge. This was the heyday of *New Society*. The Central Statistical Office launched *Social Trends* in the 1970s – I used to attend its annual press conference along with national newspaper correspondents and broadcasters – our editors were deeply interested in its results. But big institutional questions were not answered. One was about commissioning knowledge. Anticipating the market doctrines encased in new public management, Lord Rothschild said government knew approximately where it wanted knowledge – to enhance innovation and economic growth – and it should be a customer; contractors (research councils) would supply it (CPRS, 1971). Part of the agenda was corralling Rothschild's fellow FRSs – 'the powerful interest group of scientists, with their well-known lack of concern for the practical applications of additions to pure knowledge' (Shonfield, 1981: 18). It says a lot about the mindset of Whitehall and Westminster that, eight years old, the SSRC was simply ignored; social science was not science for Rothschild's purposes and was left out. But the market model for social sciences at least deserved discussion. If research was, as Shonfield said, necessarily 'a joint product of customer and contractor', where did the Council fit – a marriage broker, cuckold, or itself a customer?

Before Labour lost power in 1970, education minister Shirley Williams had said it was extraordinary that major decisions about social programmes could be made without preliminary research or attempts to evaluate them (quoted in Thomas, 1985: 3): this was why Labour had created the SSRC. (Williams later demonstrated, predictably, that practising politicians don't follow their own precepts: she led the Liberal Democrats in the House of Lords into supporting what became the 2012 Health and Social Care Act, a programme for which no 'preliminary research' had been done; the evaluation of it, if it is ever done, will show it to be a great example of faith (ideology) based law making.) But within months of her remarks, a distinct note of disappointment was being sounded. On one side it was 'the sheer intractability of many social problems ... and the complexities of intervening in the political process' (Bulmer, 1978: 23). Government demands for 'social intelligence' were being met by others. The Central Statistical Office dreamt of creating a unified and coherent set of social indicators. The SSRC became 'somewhat distanced from practical policy-making, is not concerned with specific problem-solving research but more with basic research. Its funds tend to be devoted to this and to strategic research and it applies disciplinary and theoretical considerations in judging the allocation of resources' (Bulmer, 1978: 40). His judgement is all the more striking when, at the time, the SSRC was funding panels on drug addiction, on central-local government relationships, children in care, accountability in education, energy research, North Sea oil, pre-school education, and micro computers in schools. Which prompts the question: why did such 'application' produce so little apparent 'impact'? Patricia Thomas was herself a commissioner of research as deputy director of the Nuffield Foundation and in the mid-1980s reviewed a set of studies in housing, education and employment that came on stream between 1968 and 1970. She concluded that 'it remains commonplace for policy decisions to be uninformed by research' (Thomas, 1985: 4). SSRC research had not been 'ameliorative'. Some was not good, lacked authority; most did not penetrate to those who might use it. Fortuitously it might chime with what ministers and civil servants were proposing to do anyway and acquired marginal value as affirmation or as legitimating.

By the mid-1970s, the Council had become more or less become what it remains – a means of channelling public money to support universities, but presented as support of a knowledge base. The dual support through the higher education budget, administered by the University Grants Committee and now the funding councils layered more ambiguity over the Council's role. Was it to supplement, complement other funding of social science, or the inverse?

As for the position of the SSRC in relation to the great debates of the era, it's hard not to conclude that it was marginal. On the size of the state, the effectiveness of tax policy (Labour introduced a wealth tax in circumstances of deep disagreement), the power of the unions and the balance of the economy, the SSRC was hard to profile. It paid for research, on class, employment relations and so on, but the results stayed below the radar. A watershed moment was the launch of a right-wing assault on the public sector by economists and the *Sunday Times* (not yet owned by Rupert Murdoch). The UK had 'too few producers' and a bloated state (Bacon and Eltis, 1976). This analysis anticipated the picture of economies being weighed down and stopped from growing by high levels of sovereign debt; this was equally tendentious and empirically dubious (Reinhart and Rogoff, 2009). The burgeoning literature in the 1970s about national decline was, of course, inflected by social science, but not SSRC social science. The Centre for Studies in Social Policy enjoyed a brilliant few years under Rudolf Klein and Janet Lewis, analysing spending and social policy with influence and distinction and supported by foundations and its own efforts. Its success prompted a late '70s debate about the creation of a 'British Brookings', to be paid for in part by the Ford Foundation; the London School of Economics offered a home. But its manifesto (Dahrendorf, 1995b: 490) had poignant echoes of what Young and Shonfield had wanted for the SSRC. Of course researchers and projects supported by the SSRC had both intellectual and policy influence, as analysts sought to understand the changing contours of class, party affiliation, industrial and urban structure, but it is hard – 40 years on – to swallow a sense that this critical period, when keys turned in so many locks, was under-served by contemporary social science.

ASSASSINATION

The attempt made by the Thatcher government to destroy the SSRC reads, nowadays, as both extraordinary and banal. Quangos come and go. I worked for one, the Audit Commission, which was despatched during the summer break by a minister and his special advisers after the most minimal consultation. But the assault on the SSRC was remarkable, for its whiff of Kulturkampf – an unBritish example of partisanship suppressing due process. There were even elements of Stalinism, some said, for where outside the Soviet Union would a government punish science for coming up with the wrong answer to Keith Joseph's questions about transmitted deprivation? The Thatcher government held to a complex and far from consistent political ideology – which did not stop social scientists (including many funded by the survivor research council) carrying on claiming politics was convergent and increasingly ideology free.

Money came first. The SSRC's real-term budget was cut by a quarter in the three years after 1979; during the 1980s the number of doctoral students supported fell by three quarters (Halsey, 2004: 137). Joseph had reasons to look askance at the SSRC. Many of its practitioners held views of the world he rejected; by now he had redefined his political project as their extirpation. Education, in particular, 'had come to be strongly infused by anarchism and Marxism initially, feminism and anti-racism later' (Hammersley, 2002: 2) – though the author of that quote calls them 'radical ideas' rather than ideologies. Already, as a shadow minister in the '60s, Joseph had told the chair of the SSRC it was packed with leftists (Shonfield, 1975: 7). He had a point, though Andrew Shonfield, taking him through the list of names, found Joseph could not supply chapter and verse. He might have cited David Donnison's contemporaneous account of research for policy, in which he characterised the Fabian Society as the spiritual centre of social policy research (Donnison in Bulmer, 1978: 57).

Joseph announced his conversion from conservatism to a pro-market philosophy after the Tories lost power in 1974. Collectivists (social scientists were implicated) had resisted capitalism and dragged Britain down the path towards decline and permissiveness, in popular culture, behaviour and lax financial discipline leading to inflation – a monetary phenomenon. Joseph of course drew on social science. On arriving at trade and industry in 1979 he suggested his civil servants read a list of books he handed them, starting, of course, with Friedrich von Hayek.

Yet Joseph, as Secretary for Health and Social Security in the Heath government, had turned to the SSRC as the means of addressing what he considered an emergent social policy problem, the persistence of poverty in a society where general standards of living were rising. Empirical research has since amply and additionally disconfirmed the idea of a lump of deprivation moving remorselessly through the bloodline of poor families. The poor are always with us – though neither Joseph nor his Tory successors were keen on the relativity of poverty in an increasingly affluent society – but people enter and leave the population who are poor (Hills, 2014). But Joseph was right in believing today's poor are linked (causally) with tomorrow's. The evidence, as read by Gregg and Machin (1998), shows not only that children who grow up poor are more likely to do less well later in life, but there is also a degree of 'intergenerational transmission': these people's children are also more likely to experience poorer outcomes. Joseph had a point, too, about what Tories like to call character – others might prefer something like a higher quality of relationship between parents and children, allowing or pushing the children to break free of constraining social circumstances. But some children can and do overcome unfavourable early circumstances to find happiness and success in later life.

If Joseph took against the SSRC partly because of the way social scientists had handled his notion of transmitted deprivation – the subject of a major, decade-long research programme – what he did not realise was how close the SSRC's leaders and he were to being on the same page. It was not that Robin Matthews, Derek Robinson or Michael Posner, the SSRC chairs in post as the programme unfolded, agreed with him about the alleged phenomenon. What the SSRC leadership regretted was how recalcitrant academic social scientists were in responding to a bona fide question from politics and how reluctant to proffer to Joseph not confirmation but a practical response that might have gone along these lines – no, not that, but try this formula for understanding and addressing the issue. (The formula would, in the era of Tory government, necessarily need to stop short of recommending the replacement of capitalism or severely redistributive taxation but – eyeing Joseph's own record – family income supplement or tax credits might have been acceptable.) Posner said no one could read the summary of findings without 'some increase in their knowledge' but gloomily added that 'what is to be done as a result is a far more delicate matter', knowing that after a decade civil servants and ministers wanted something more than additional 'material for argument and debate' (Posner, 1982).

The story of attempted abolition after the Tories took power in 1979 illustrates the usual infirmities and contingencies of government. The Treasury's permission was necessary. The chancellor, Sir Geoffrey Howe, had earlier in his career been keenly interested in social problems and research to elucidate them. But the SSRC was an expedient sacrifice and it is notable that ministers did not hear Sir Robin Butler or other civil service panjandrums speaking up in its favour. Unlike Eric Pickles and the Audit Commission, Joseph felt he needed the cover of an inquiry and Victor Rothschild was an obvious candidate: a biologist, sufficiently Tory friendly and eminent.

Rothschild's report reeks of intellectual condescension (Rothschild, 1982) but, amid the jibes, sarcasm and world-weary self-regard, he stuck with the view that some mechanism was needed to support a distinct body of work, and the research council was it. The science establishment, with which he shared views critical of the intellectual quality of much social science, was willing to rely on the judgement of an FRS. Rothschild threw one-liners to the gallery on sociology and the SSRC's administrative costs and opened the way for the Tories to flog a hobbyhorse in the shape of allegedly marxisant SSRC research on industrial relations. (Marxists, of course, were highly suspicious of trade unions. Sir Kenneth Berrill, an establishment economist, gave the SSRC research unit at the University of Warwick a clean bill of health.)

Thatcher herself had other fish to fry and played no distinct role, unlike Joseph's special adviser Oliver Letwin, who was despatched to ferret through SSRC documents to find the smoking gun (Flather in Bulmer, 1987: 363).

Paul Flather, a journalist on the *Times Higher Education Supplement*, concludes that pressure from social science as an organised interest group was a negligible factor in the reprieve. It was, more or less, a matter of establishment inertia and Joseph's lack of political staying power. For the Thatcher cabinet the fate of the SSRC was a peripheral matter compared with dealing with local government, the burgeoning bill for welfare as unemployment grew and, within months, the Falklands crisis.

Joseph was defeated, but no one paid much attention. Council folklore sees the reprieve as a watershed. The ESRC, rechristened, became more professional, relocated to a business park in Swindon and – allegedly – became more attuned to government and business. In fact, few if any of the ambiguities in the knowledge economy were resolved. Administratively, the council became more cautious, more civil service like. Its capacity to think for itself rather than function as an intermediary between Whitehall and universities diminished.

A COUNTERFACTUAL: WHAT IF ASSASSINATION HAD TAKEN PLACE?

In a parallel universe, Rothschild could have found reasons to say the SSRC's disappearance was justified. Whitehall departments could pick up work relevant to their profiles; the Advisory Board for the Research Councils could take on foresight and futures work needing social science input; the UGC could expand its grants to universities to support research, including the data archive and other infrastructure; the British Academy or even the Department for Education could administer postgraduate grants. Joseph had never rejected the need for such functions, which would have been easy to rebrand without using the dread phrase 'social science'.

In what ways would the intellectual landscape have been left barren by the non-commissioning of work that the ESRC went on to instigate? At its starkest, would the poor be worse off, the UK more unequal, banking executives any less likely to overreach and crash the financial system? In real political time, would the absence of the ESRC have prevented Nigel Lawson shadowing the Deutschmark, the UK's brief alignment with the Exchange Rate Mechanism, non-participation in the Euro, the collapse of manufacturing, property inflation, mass migration, the uneven but unmistakable advance of women in the workplace, education and culture? But that's to anticipate a reckoning we have to attempt in Chapter 8.

One thing we can probably say in this counterfactual is that certain disciplines, notably sociology, perhaps also anthropology and social policy, would have fared less well – unless they had changed their spots. Even this is not assured. The Thatcher Tories, as under Major and Cameron, said they were interested in social mobility, though they did not fund a 1980's cohort study. Say the SSRC's budget had been in part redistributed to departments. The Home Office had never conceded much to the SSRC and retained a strong role as commissioner of research on crime, both from its own staff and its academic networks. It might have funded more. Perhaps Council-sponsored research did 'shape' (public and policy) consciousness, which changed behaviour or attitudes. The evidence from contemporary historical study is sketchy. What, in retrospect, is hard to do is to connect any given volume of research spend to outputs and – a theme of this book – any given 'level' of research to explanation, and certainly not to the predictability of events, or trends.

4

REPRIEVE AND NORMALISATION

SUMMARY

Rebranded, the ESRC nestled into the research council system while cleverly adapting to new government emphases on utility – the 'priorities' assumed by the council were far from onerous or injurious to academic autonomy. But assimilation to 'science' further emphasised the council's distance from policy making under both the Major and Blair governments and the parochialism of UK social science in wider debates about the domain's future.

After the climacteric, the research council took a new name, slimmed administration and, after one or two hiccups, fell in with the Thatcher government's sketchy and limited plans for decentralising Whitehall. It was a kind of resurrection, and credit must be given to the Essex University specialist on rural labour, Howard Newby who became executive chair in 1988, though his predecessor Sir Douglas Hague had steadied the ship. (Hague was a Thatcherite who believed in the need for social research, especially on communications technology, innovation and performance enhancement.) Business and lay people formed a slightly greater proportion of members of the council. By the end of the decade finance – postgraduate training had taken the hit rather than research – had even begun to recover.

The history of the social sciences since 1965 has two axes. One is assimilation to 'science'; the other is demonstrating 'use' or impact. Social sciences had oscillated, pushed (since Heyworth) by the drive to rationalise social policy:

> Their fortunes have also been dependent upon arrangements for coordinated science and technology policy. But significantly, neither the documents that set out the principles of science policy for the 1960s and 1970s (Trend, Rothschild), nor the arrangements in which they came to be embodied, paid them any attention. By the end of the 1970s, both coordinated social policy and coordinated science policy had been superseded. (Blume, 1987: 84)

But that left space for the ESRC to insert itself into 'science' as a sort of willing adept, winning acceptance at the Advisory Board for the Research Councils and laying the groundwork for later chief executives of the ESRC to become major players, after the ABRC became RCUK. For example, it jumped adroitly on the bandwagon rolling from the late 1980s to establish interdisciplinary research centres – such as what became the Institute for Social and Economic Research (ISER) at the University of Essex. The social science take was to expand the field for inductivism, amassing large data sets. ISER started as the ESRC Research Centre on Micro-Social Change, which covered a large waterfront; it launched the British Household Panel Study, now Understanding Society, which offered the means of studying relationships, but only retrospectively (ISER, n.d.). Later, Sir Ian Diamond and his successor Paul Boyle became RCUK workhorses; Diamond's great coup was to win system approval in defining ESRC spending as capital investment – not laboratories or Antarctic ships, but data sets. They understood that the ESRC could secure cover by becoming a loyal subordinate of 'science' while adopting language and posture to convince ministers (if they cared to look) that this research council was also 'useful'.

Newby had seen at close quarters, in 1994, how valuable such cover can be (Donovan, 2001: 292). The ESRC proposed to join a consortium to look at British sexual attitudes and behaviour – not before time, as the Aids epidemic gathered strength. Perhaps a worldly-wise chair (or council) would have rung alarm bells or sought to palliate ministers. As it turned out, the ESRC was left holding responsibility for a project that Number 10 disapproved of. Adroit footwork by Newby and the willingness of the Wellcome Trust to step in and pay for the project meant that it went ahead without embarrassment. Political attitudes to sexual disclosure in surveys subsequently changed, in a liberal direction.

Awareness of such dangers encouraged a kind of parochialism. Formerly, Council chiefs had played in the big league, hobnobbing with ministers and permanent secretaries roughly as equals, despite political differences. Now they retreated to the bunker and recast themselves as academics. Big debates about the identity of the social sciences – notably the Gulbenkian Commission (Wallerstein et al., 1996) – passed the UK by. What is striking, in hindsight, is how rich the 'social science' conversation had been in the late 1960s and 1970s. Later, disciplinary particularity asphyxiated wider debate. The ESRC did not challenge the academic dynamic that sliced and diced knowledge into specialist chunks, guarded by peers. Early optimism was long since dissipated. 'Our lack of understanding of social processes is even greater than our lack of knowledge of social conditions, and this lack of understanding may be greatest in the identification of aspects of process which are malleable by policy', two distinguished analysts concluded a year after the reprieve, in a book dripping with pessimism about both social science and policy making (Hogwood and Peters, 1985: 21).

They might have had in mind the absence of the ESRC, as the Thatcher and Major governments undertook big shifts in policy. An example is the Next Steps programme, by which chunks of administrative work were 'hived off' into freestanding agencies. It did not happen like that, but here was an example of a highly theoretical, conceptually dense piece of policymaking … in which UK social science played no discernible part. Next Steps – according to a contemporary analyst – was 'grounded in theory'; it drew on public choice doctrine and theories of principal-agent (Greer, 1994). It is not that UK social scientists were not looking at the phenomenon, but they were after the event observers for the most part, not involved. Managerial 'reform' is an example of the impotence and passivity of English-speaking social science in the UK against American free market doctrine. This said 'welfare' was maximised through the operations of markets, from which government and political will should be excluded. If government had to exist, best to devolve its functions to arm's-length, expert-led bodies such as central banks or even (as proposed in the UK) autonomous bodies to decide on the tax take and fiscal policy. Social scientists were tempted, for weren't they the experts who could say with exquisite precision whether a fraction of a percentage point change in interest rates would raise or lower the rate of inflation?

These were years when much social science supplied justification to dominant politics; the Council was either complicit (in funding it) or absent (preferring to keep its head down). The relative lack of attention paid to fiscal affairs meant the ESRC was not implicated in the debacle over the poll tax (Butler et al., 1994). Poll tax is often cited as a great blunder. It's an 'obvious example' of where social science could have identified bad policy long before it is inflicted on the public (Binmore, 2003: xviii). But I cannot recall the ESRC or indeed social scientists pressing the Thatcher government to change its ways.

It's notable how, with the exception of sex, the ESRC avoided controversy during the years after the climacteric. Instead it became normal, and disappeared. Rothschild had criticised its bureaucracy and the new body had to prove itself leaner and fitter. One way was to leave London. Did it affect the quality of staff over subsequent years? Decentralisation is a policy that could benefit from social science analysis. With the ONS, relocation to Newport in South Wales (parts of the ONS were already outside London) has been blamed for lost quality in its work, good statisticians said to be difficult to recruit in or to

South Wales. The ESRC was dispersed to a business park near the railway station in Swindon; it's an open question whether it has had any effect on the calibre of staff. There was an immediate instance of recruitment being affected. Douglas Hague's appointed successor was the planner and urbanist Peter Hall, later knighted. On realising he himself would be expected to relocate, this expert in dispersal demurred, which opened the space for Newby (who arrived after an interregnum and a mutually educative interview with the Tory Education Secretary Kenneth Baker).

From the mid-1990s, the governance of the organisation changed to bring it into line with the conventional quango model of lay chair and full-time chief executive. The model works best when the chair can bring political connexions and protective networks. The ESRC has not been blessed. Its chairs in recent times have been off the political pace, with the exception of Adair Turner (appointed chair in 2007) – but he lasted only a matter of months, before relinquishing the role to work on climate change, then on the salvation of capitalism from itself. While chief executives, with exceptions, have done well in terms of networking and liaison with other research councils and higher education, they have tended not to be 'Whitehall warriors'. The Turner episode is a might have been. He was a potential social science strategist in the mould of Shonfield. Had he stayed, would he have demanded the ESRC carry through the necessary 'fundamental challenge to recent conventional wisdom' (Cassidy, 2009: 361)?

Newby left the ESRC not to run a department, agency or large local authority, nor to head a firm or significant non-profit but (as it appeared) to return to the bosom of higher education, becoming vice chancellor of Southampton University. That is not to query Newby's talents, recognised by his later appointments as chief executive of the Higher Education Funding Council for England and vice chancellor of Liverpool University. It was none the less a pointer to the identity of the research council. His successor, from 1994, was a Birmingham University professor who, given his subject matter – Soviet politics – might have been an adept at the arts of government, but instead led the ESRC to a place somewhere outside the mainstream. Successive leaders never managed to lodge it in the 'indispensable' category, as adjudicated by the Treasury or ministers.

As long ago as 1968 permanent secretaries were complaining about social science jargon and impenetrability; Rothschild had added his pennyworth. Now, under an imaginative communications director, Tim Whitaker, the ESRC began insisting that grant holders acquired some minimal competence in dealing with the media as it started to use available channels with more energy. (The Programme on Information and Communication Technologies, launched in 1985, was one of the first to be allotted funds to undertake dissemination – but people appointed to the role tended to be librarians.) An effort was made to encourage outreach and to equip and motivate academic social scientists to become more 'engaged' – the rise of that word to today's status as indispensable cliché began then.

KEEPING ITS DISTANCE

Newby and his successor positioned the ESRC as an enthusiast for 'use', in terms set out by the Major government in 1993 (White Paper, 1993). This focused on the poor uptake of research in the UK, and (the Major government in power) instead of asking about the structure of British business and boardroom attitudes and competence, required the research councils to do more to meet the needs of users and beneficiaries. Once again, social science was not on the official radar. But the ESRC reorganised accordingly. It would still give out grants 'responsively', but some two-thirds of its activities would be aligned with 'themes' that (viewed in a certain light) looked like they were attuned to the worries of the political class and (if it were ever to think collectively) business. Allocating research to themes became a fine art.

On close examination these 'research priorities' were not so obtrusive. For example, 2003's iteration started with (the need to understand) 'the forces that influence economic performance and development in an international and comparative context' (ESRC, 2004). The Blair government's political and intellectual capital was heavily invested in the beneficence of globalisation and, in the absence of a full-throated social science critique, which was never on the cards, it was inevitable the ESRC would adopt such a theme, which could cover everything and nothing. As it turned out, financialisation – one of those 'forces' – was never understood or its malign effects predicted, with results we now live with.

Next came 'the complex relationship between people and the environment', a commitment of surpassing blandness that indicated no more than that this (or any conceivable) research council would pay attention to sustainability, whether or not deputy prime ministers were jetting off to summits in Rio or requiring English councils to produce statements of their sustainability work. The next theme was 'the nature of governance in a changing world', followed by 'how knowledge is acquired, valued, communicated and applied' and 'life course, lifestyles and health'. These covered the waterfront. The theme 'social stability and exclusion' (the forces shaping society and the implications for social stability) did echo language used by the Blairites, who banned poverty in favour of exclusion. The remaining themes were 'the nature of work and the factors that underlie the success of business and organisations' – the golden question, answering which would make social scientists rich and famous – and the domestic issue, 'the strength of skills, resources and methods in UK social science'.

Pointing to such thematic priorities, academic critics say the ESRC moved to fund only research that was 'relevant', especially to government. The trouble with the thesis is that it requires the state (ministers) to know what they want or, a more sophisticated variant, the research council to be sufficiently politicised to anticipate what they want.

AT THE HEART OF THE STATE

In the 1990s, with the Tories solidly in power, the ESRC undertook two major programmes in areas touching the very heart of the state, on devolution and constitutional change and on Whitehall and the civil service. The first, like the Future of Scotland programme described in the preceding chapter, showed the ESRC anticipating discussions that took flight later, some only two decades on. It involved a set of grants for studies of the constituent countries of the UK, their polities and constitutional futures. Unusually, the governance around the programme was not academic-dominated but had as chair the journalist and later think-tanker Peter Riddell and others, myself included. This was not work the government or opposition especially wanted done. Although when it came to power in 1997 the Labour government embarked on an extensive measure of devolution, the then leader of the opposition Tony Blair was far from committed and Labour was doing little fresh thinking, certainly not of a kind that amounted to demands for knowledge from the ESRC. If the programme raises another question – how far work done in era 'lasts' into another, when political and institutional circumstances are much changed – it certainly did not show the ESRC as the cat's paw of the state.

With the Whitehall programme, the ESRC might have been doing ministers' bidding by scoping modernisation and reform at the heart of the state. Instead, at the fag end of the era of Tory dominance, the Thatcherite reform drive of the 1980s was spent. The Major government continued privatising and contracting out, without much regard for 'evidence', but in structural reform there was little interest. The Labour opposition largely accepted the institutional status quo, as it did on taking office in 1997.

The programme was led by a political scientist, Rod Rhodes, determined to prove various theses – such as the 'hollowing out of the state'. The civil service itself, under Cabinet Secretary Robin Butler, was politely accommodating and utterly uninterested. It wasn't obstruction, merely indifference. The programme had minimal impact. It's hard now to recollect a single piece of analysis that lasted. A prevalent idea, then and still, was 'overload' – but that had come from studies a decade or so previously, many of them American and free-market inflected. Overload itself faded as an idea, curiously irrelevant to day-to-day politics, which since 2010 has been about shrinking the state – a cure (albeit drastic) for the state allegedly doing too much.

Whatever the quality of the social science in such programmes, the point is that here was the ESRC doing what it said on the tin and autonomously providing for research that might in other circumstances have been especially relevant to users or policy makers. But in fact, as so often, it failed to secure lodgement in political or administrative consciousness.

WHERE'S THE CAUSAL FORMULA?

On coming to power, some Labour ministers started querying the knowledge base for the interventions they proposed. Which were, naturally intended to be ameliorative. New Labour anxiety was particularly acute over education. Under Blair, Labour had made the ideological commitment to downplay redistribution in favour of accentuating mobility through opportunity. That (the doctrine said) would come through better schooling for the poor and disadvantaged. What, asked Education Secretary David Blunkett, were the causal formulae on which he should base projected changes to class sizes, curriculum or teachers' salaries (Blunkett, 2000)?

Blunkett's frustration reflected a prevalent view among civil servants in the social policy departments – the permanent Secretary in Education and Employment was Michael Bichard, a formidable public official who had been successively chief executive in local authorities and headed the Benefits Agency, and served on ESRC committees. Blunkett said he wanted more research relevant 'to the real debates that affect people's life chances'. He wanted causality. 'We are not interested in worthless correlations based on small samples from which it is impossible to draw generalisable conclusions.' What surprised many was that Blunkett had obviously given some thought to the knowledge economy, at least in education, and was using methodological language few ministers ever used.

Critics responded with an observation that can be made of all ministers: did he really want evidence that might disprove or undermine what he (and his Sheffield constituents) believed to be the case? The problem became clearer when Blunkett moved to the Home Office and flatly rejected studies of anti-social behaviour – another shibboleth of the Blair years. But a more troubling response was that causal modelling of the kind Blunkett wanted in education did not exist, though official social science (the ESRC included) had never admitted it. Social science, well or badly funded depending on your view, had not produced such goods. Such goods probably did not exist. Labour complaints were, however, accompanied by growth in budgets and general support from ministers for more social inquiry and evaluation, and the issue went away.

Given the fate of the Labour government and its policy hits and misses (Toynbee and Walker, 2010), it's easy to effect condescension. But the group around Blair did aspire to utilise knowledge, to undergird their reforming intentions (albeit while sticking to the Tories' spending targets) with evidence. What they missed was a sense they were being met half way. That's not to say the ESRC wasn't supporting Richard Layard's work on subjective wellbeing and echoing ministers' interest in social capital then, later, behavioural economics and 'nudge'. The head of the policy unit, Geoff Mulgan, formerly of Demos, the think tank, was anything but unlearned or unsophisticated in thinking about knowledge and power. I recall a conversation with him inside Number 10, sitting on a chintz sofa in the warren of rooms that make up the centre of UK government, hearing him complain about gaps and absences, unconvinced that the knowledge they needed was forthcoming. In retrospect, these Labour years seem an opportunity missed:

> Mulgan bemoans the fact it only rarely gives them a sense of how the world is turning. The ESRC has done relatively well out of spending rounds but, say some, it should have done a lot better given new Labour's enthusiasm for social policy. (Walker, 2002)

This isn't to say the ESRC should have climbed into bed with the Blairites, whose priorities were necessarily ephemeral, but rather to establish itself and the social sciences it represented as the place for strategic thinking about the class of 'problem' that would still be there, under Brown, under Cameron and his successor, too. Examples are productivity, structure of corporate rewards, technical and vocational education, migration, social mobility, technological change and adaptation to it. This had been what Michael Young saw as the Council's avocation.

What happened was that Labour created knowledge for themselves. They set up a host of mini commissions of inquiry, bringing together practitioners, policy makers and, yes, academics to think through policy for youth, rough sleepers, housing, young offenders. And, in the Cabinet Office, they gave the green light to reorganising the Civil Service College into a new structure, intended to focus and channel 'useful knowledge'.

THE BLAIR ERA – MISSED OPPORTUNITIES?

Enter the ESRC, in the shape of former chief executive Ron Amann. In 1999 he was recruited as the first head of the Centre for Management and Policy Studies, with the rank of permanent secretary. This surely showed the tide was turning and the ESRC securing new recognition as an engine of precisely the useful knowledge Blunkett said the New Labour government wanted. In fact the centre of government under Blair was a mess, a confusion of units and contending mini empires. The Amann appointment was a half-hearted effort by the incumbent Cabinet Secretary Sir Richard Wilson to give the impression he was doing the Blairites' bidding, while doing as little as possible to change the culture or practice of his colleagues. That sounds cynical. In fact Wilson had other priorities, trying to placate the demands of a prime minister who himself was eager but deeply uninterested in process or structure; and dealing with foot and mouth disease. Amann was a child among brutalised adults. His fellow permanent secretaries had no intention of deferring to the CMPS; he lacked the weight and political connexions to push them. Wilson was on their side. Whatever Geoff Mulgan and others in Number 10 envisaged for knowledge for government, they could not avoid the inevitable, which was the consignment of CPMS to Whitehall's equivalent of the Siberian power station.

The Blair government proceeded, as its successors did, to make random use of both internally generated research and what social science inquiry showed. Where it did not suit – especially in criminal justice – it was ignored. No advances were made in clarifying the respective roles of in-house and research council work. Evidence institutions were created, notably the National Institute of Clinical Excellence, now the National Institute for Health and Care Excellence.

After Amann, the system chose as his successor another professor, the sociologist Gordon Marshall. On his departure, in 2005, he became vice chancellor of the University of Reading, just as his two successors left to head universities. The first of them, Ian Diamond, was a social statistician and demographer; the next a geographer. All were able, but all distinctly academic in their background and networks. This insulation of the ESRC meant that the change of government in 2010 caused barely a ripple on the surface of the ESRC's external relationships; a minus was its relative insignificance as the principal provider of social science as great battles raged about finance, macroeconomic policy in recession, the nature and persistence of poverty. Britain is broken, declared the Tory leader David Cameron in 2008. Did social science concur? The ESRC took no corporate view.

Yet it had commissioned the data that would, sooner or later, confirm the contention – assuming 'broken' could be given some measurable definition. The decade from 2000 had been fat years for social research. The ESRC launched a new birth cohort study with the blessing of ministers, tracking children born at the millennium and in 2008 expanded the British Household Panel Survey into a new programme, intending to revisit the same families from then on – with financial assistance from government departments, whose own research budgets were expanding. These studies became one of the ESRC's strongest calling cards both in Whitehall and as 'science'. They demanded quantitative skills and a distinct social science methodology to do with sampling, interviewing and interpretation. Perhaps it was inevitable that successive chief executives of the ESRC were themselves experts in handling big data sets.

5

AN AGENT OF AMELIORATION

SUMMARY

High hopes for impact on policy accompanied the research council's birth: it was to be an agent of social, economic and political amelioration. The research council was intended to provide 'policy science', instruments for better control of individual and collective destiny. Academic suppliers of knowledge demurred, resenting requirements then and now to show 'impact'. What are the implications for research governance if knowledge for action is inherently 'situationist' and contextual?

The early days were Wordsworthian. Bliss it was to be alive, but to be young ... The Heyworth Committee, the Labour politicians who enacted its recommendations and the first movers and shakers in the SSRC were broadly agreed: this was about creating knowledge that would modernise and improve Britain. The Council would be an agent of amelioration. With that went – and still goes – a conviction that social science is positivist in the uncomplicated sense that it can analyse events and predict outcomes with more success than the statesman or man of affairs. The conviction is 'indispensable to [the] claim to give advice that is worth listening to' (Kaysen, 1968: 94).

The backdrop to the creation of the SSRC was

> the implicit assumption that political consensus made it possible to seek technical (institutional, organisational and administrative) solutions to Britain's social and economic problems. It is no accident that as people celebrated the end of ideology (possibly prematurely) they were also celebrating the birth of rationality in policy making (perhaps prematurely too). (Challis et al., 1988: 13)

Social scientists have not given much thought to the converse: if it's not linear, not positive and we don't predict, what is it. Telling power holders 'it's more complicated than you thought' may be necessary, but surely as a tactic, not an objective.

For the ESRC, the question needs to be phrased slightly differently, since official social science can never admit to the non-linear (let alone the anti-linear) case. If what the ESRC funds is *fundamental, background or contextual*, the explanations it will come up with, sooner or later, must in some sense be *better, deeper, more satisfying* than the quick and dirty work being done by non-academics. That's the theme of this chapter.

THE GAP

'Positive' and 'linear' imply the existence of an agent (the state) creating and/or deploying knowledge for public betterment. Such a belief belongs squarely within the tradition of political thought that sees the necessity and may even extol collective agency (the state). The SSRC did indeed have a distinctly social democratic colouring. In his foreword to one edition of the SSRC Newsletter (Crosland, 1975), Environment Secretary Tony Crosland said the housing conditions of many were an affront. Such an exclamation passed without notice. Both the problem and the belief that research would help progressive politicians such as him ameliorate them were embedded in conventional wisdom – what Keith Joseph was determined to smash. As Education Secretary in the previous Wilson government, Crosland had backed the SSRC's creation and installed Michael Young as first chair in their shared belief that (social) knowledge was – inherently – beneficial to (social) causes. This overlapped, in an age looking forward with confidence, with the belief that social science gave us a lien on the future, helping us to improve life tomorrow. An unstated but important corollary was that social scientist and minister had a lot in common, including values and general political outlook.

It's hard to swallow an acute sense of bright hopes rapidly tarnished, then more or less discarded. One of Young's first acts had been to establish the Next Thirty Years Committee, its members including Richard Lipsey, the Essex economist and author of a widely used textbook, *Positive Economics* (note the title), the social psychologist Marie Jahoda (the SSRC's only woman) and the future General Secretary of the Trades Union Congress Len Murray.

The author of *The Rise of the Meritocracy* was hardly a naive optimist but he confidently predicted decision makers would demand more and more assistance from social scientists in scoping and forecasting – in planning economic growth, energy demand, volumes of road traffic, school places, building New Towns, providing for leisure (the working week was sure to shrink), training tomorrow's doctors and so on. What would Young and Shonfield have made of the Office of Budget Responsibility and its intriguing forays into the future course of spending? If not a research council responsibility, surely fiscal dimensions should be tied in with its 'projective' work. Young edited a collection of essays on forecasting which, in those unexclusive and undisciplined days, could even include an essay from a private sector professional, David Grove of Shankland, Cox and Associates. In that collection, you hear the decade's faith in the state, in planning and in the capacity of social science. On its purpose, there was no question. 'The social sciences are and will be useful and in that measure supported in so far as they add to mankind's span of control' (Young, 1968: 20). Note that word – control. How antipathetic modern social scientists find it, even those uncontaminated by post-modernism. Young was simultaneously sceptical about relying on hypothetico-deductive models and supremely confident that by studying socio-economic dynamics it would turn up 'regularities' permitting reasonably confident forecasts of what might lie ahead. Young proposed a 'clearing house' for social science forecasts, making them more readily available to companies, local authorities and planners. You can smile at the forecasts that proved plain wrong – especially those on land use, income growth, retirement age and the work-leisure balance. But belief in the ameliorative powers of social science analysis is compelling. That was what the SSRC was for. Ironically Young's clearing house idea was taken up, and it turned out you could make money from it. In 1974 the Henley Centre for Forecasting was founded as a social enterprise, then successfully sold analysis and futurology.

How quickly the mood darkened and bright hopes dimmed. 'Ambitions and expectations have become distinctly more modest: the experience of the 1970s has caused us to re-evaluate the contribution that the social sciences make', wrote the secretary to the Heyworth Committee (Cherns, 1979: xvi). What went wrong? To reply blandly and patronisingly that Young and the early Council leaders were naive, misunderstanding the prospects and possibilities of social science, won't do, because condemning them is to pass adverse judgement on a belief that continues to this day. Jane Lewis says Heyworth misunderstood that the social problems he listed were 'social constructions and profoundly context dependent' (Lewis, n.d.). But if social science knows its answers have to be time-specific, institutional and – a key additional attribute – arrived at in the sight and hearing of problem-practitioners, why has it persisted to make claims on public resource as if its knowledge base were nomothetic?

Young's phrase 'span of control' conforms to Enlightenment ideas of science: to know is to empower action and pursue the project of better self- and collective management. That implies a fair degree of symmetry – even sympathy – between scientist and actor (chief executive, permanent secretary – or insurgent shop steward or recalcitrant rate payer). But, only partly recognised by Young, research council knowledge is usually unbranded, not readily differentiated from other streams of understanding. How special is it? The status of 'scientific knowledge' is based on claims of procedure, openness to peer scrutiny, debate and contestation. Does it follow that other types of knowing are thereby relegated to a subordinate position?

THE POOL OF KNOWLEDGE

The Heyworth Committee never quite got to grips with the different forms information and analysis for decision making could take, especially the gap between academy knowledge and the data and analysis underpinning practice. British institutional development took place in relative isolation from American debates, particularly active in the 1960s. Americans had identified, for example, the importance of intermediaries between researchers and ministers, committee chairmen and officials who implement policy. But where might such 'policy intellectuals' sit; which institutions should do policy analysis? Could it be done inside government, in think tanks and autonomous research institutes as well as in universities? Much social science inflected work was already being done in and by departments and agencies, and local government, creating (already) 'a research apparatus of bewildering complexity' (Thomas, 1985).

Young, a networker, partially solved the problem through his personal connections. Suppers with Tony Crosland and Chelly Halsey went quite a way to bridge the gap. Where research rubbed shoulders with policy making, social science and its research council would be listened to. But Young's successors were not all plugged in. As we have seen they became increasingly decoupled from power, more academic. Ministers change. The research council's half-century saw Tories in power for 27 years, during which their ideological attachment to the state sharply diminished. But ideology aside, the question was whether academic research produced 'useful' knowledge and whether the research council had any role in filtering or channelling the turbid waters of the great pool of potential knowledge for policy and practice in which decision makers swam, the products of its own funding forming only one of the tributaries. The analogy of a pool is helpful because it can be seen as a reservoir of past research findings as well as a place into which new streams of knowledge flow. It facilitates the possibility of a dynamic interrogation between accumulated knowledge and the policy and practice issues of the day. At its 25th anniversary Howard Newby said social science had 'seeped into the conventional wisdom'. Social science had taught that vocational training explained productivity differentials between the UK and Germany; that child abuse was more prevalent than once supposed; that small business mattered to growth and innovation (Newby, 1990). But these instances show – the pool simile – how mixed knowledge can be. German vocational training was identified in the 19th century and has played a part in debates since; child abuse is a public anxiety fanned by media; small business is rhetorical protection for corporate interests. Seepage may take time; knowledge gets buffeted by winds of contingency. The year before Newby's remarks, the ESRC had summarised results from a study of urban and regional change, stating: 'Northern cities have no choice but to raise their international economic profile if they are to participate in recovery' (ESRC, 1989). Well, some 'chose' not to; for those that did, notably Manchester, it took long years, terrorism, popular cultural fashion and, eventually, George Osborne to get there.

The half-century has been marked by sporadic and agonistic debate about the 'instrumentality' of research. Here is a representative statement of the academic case. 'As publicly funded researchers, we clearly have a responsibility to contribute something in return to society – in other words, there is some form of a social contract that we are obliged to honour. As part of this, there is an obvious need for public accountability' (Martin, 2011: 247). The tone is grudging. How far should the research council insist on that accountability? Often social scientists resented what they saw as being under the cosh of having to account, whether to the research council or to university funders, whether the rubric was 'evidence' or 'impact'.

IMPACT AS ACCOUNTABILITY

Social scientists are prone to dismiss research assessment as a manifestation of neo-liberalism. It may be, but that still leaves publicly funded research carrying some obligation to report (in public hearing); why should academics (who possess cultural power) be any more exempt from external scrutiny than other professional interests? Yet academics, with some (often marginal) participation by policy people and other users of research, have been allowed to judge their own impact. As a result, interactive models of policy and decision making are downplayed (even though empirical evidence supports them). REF 2014 endorses a simplistic linear model, focusing on how researchers market their findings and the researcher's own role in the policy process, rather than the dynamics of the process itself.

The institutionalisation of impact in REF 2014 – which is the same as saying its academisation (impact becomes the object of research, journal articles and grant-funding applications) – goes on. But it's a reasonable interim observation that had social science been able to realise more of the early ambitions of the SSRC, perhaps the impetus behind the demand to demonstrate impact would have been less. But social science was hamstrung by conceptual and other confusions about its relationship to practice, as the 'evidence' debate shows.

It's been skewed. Far less is known about policy makers' attitudes towards research than vice versa. We lack analysis of their interaction. Much more attention has been paid to knowledge production than consumption. From the very beginnings, the Council eschewed trying to understand the conditions in which social science knowledge might be put to use. Surprisingly little empirical work has been commissioned on policy makers and executives – in terms of their mental universe. Work by the likes of Maurice Kogan remained peripheral. Despite programmes of research on Whitehall and business, we don't know enough about how policy is actually made. Despite a large academic literature on 'evidence', the effects of academic work on policy have 'proved curiously elusive and difficult to pin down' (Bulmer, 1985: 13). One reason could be that knowledge in government is inherently 'situationist'; rationality is in permanent tension with the need to persuade, negotiate and coerce (Kogan and Henkel, 2000: 28).

The question has haunted the Council, which has convened at least one 'evidence-based policy and practice' programme. It's existential. If reason and the use of evidence prevailed, we would live in a technocracy; the chair of the ESRC would ride high. Evidence for policy runs the risk of Platonism, in which, of course, academics are the guardians. How far can and ought government be made more rational without jeopardising the (necessarily) contingent and affective elements of democracy? Politics may rarely be admirable but is always unavoidable, always owing less to reason than we might wish.

INFLUENCE IS NORMATIVE

A core purpose of a social science research organisation must be to elucidate problems of policy, to help practitioners (from business executives to teachers) do it better. But 'better' is normative. Social scientists might take offence at the idea that accomplishing their purposes should be measured by profits or share prices. Yet the public advertisement for social science – put up by the Council at least – promises to find the causes and conditions for firms' success, which must mean money.

Academic social science has been reluctant to relinquish control of what constitutes evidence. It has come to be exclusive, restricted to studies certified by academics, reviewed and approved under tight presentational criteria. Much of what government does (such as tinkering with organisations, making budgets, running the NHS) and most commercial life (corporate governance, surviving in markets, changing employment) is evidence-free in this sense. In a looser sense evidence is merely applicable knowledge. Decision makers deploy facts, commission analyses and anticipate outcomes. By averting our eyes from the multiple ways in which evidence is deployed, we may misunderstand the cognitive needs and functioning of government and executive decision makers. They use past experience, however fallible, as a guide to the future, consult rules of thumb and least worst alternatives. Consider substituting intelligence for evidence. Quarrels arise inevitably and permanently over the moment and institutions of interpretation (Hennessy, 2007).

If users (sometimes daringly referred to as 'co-producers') started specifying what they wanted to know (as opposed to what researchers thought interesting) there would be less novelty and more synthesis, more integration of knowledge across disciplines and across time. How many times, over the past half-century, have we heard calls for more systematising, more integration of what we know? Claus Moser used his presidential address to the British Association a quarter-century ago to ask for annual 'state of the nation reports on health, education, urban blight' (ESRC, 1990). Alan Wilson suggests the equivalent of a 'war room' for city planning and government … to 'provide both a common information base across departments, and a bespoke element for individual departments' (Wilson, 2010: 75). But that would demand a research council that was intimate with power and knowledge needs within Whitehall, prepared to defy the boundary between 'science' and social science and to take a comprehensive and eclectic view of knowledge for policy action.

The ESRC pays for data collection and packaging, leaving moot the question of who should take the next step and make ready for utilisation. For example, the ESRC Centre on Dynamics of Ethnicity (based at the University of Manchester) packaged ONS Census data, intending to help local authorities create their own analyses. They could, in principle, add to local knowledge about ethnic minorities' health and civic participation – provided they 'stepped down' the analysis from the high levels of abstraction used by the academics into categories useable by officers and recognisable by elected members. Much contextualisation and interpretation are needed to accommodate academic research in local areas. This second stage – filtering, reworking, localising – is far from trivial. It does not just depend on 'research' capacity within the local authority plus demand for knowledge and enthusiasm for devising and implementing policy but reciprocal recognition by the academic researchers of the local knowledge base. In a divided city such as Bradford none of this is straightforward. The vague but affecting word often used is 'engagement'. If academics engage with a place, are they prepared to make any (as they would see it) epistemological sacrifices?

There is a tremendous gap in the market for updates as well as synthesis. It gets filled by informal networking, gossip and the pages of such media as the *Guardian*. Knowledge is often best fronted and conveyed by a trusted individual, an 'expert' rather than a specialist. The boundary that separates consultancy from research is porous, marked by club affiliation and speed of delivery and in the private sector and parts of government ideological affinity with commercial consultancy firms. Knowledge becomes 'causal' through follow-up human interaction, for example through colleges and networks of the sort that do exist for research among chief police officers. The social care inspectorates do some of this; consultants ditto. Such people don't easily fit into the limited number of roles recognised by universities; the ESRC has tried to work round rigidities by creating fellowships and the like but is swimming against the tide. Involving users in framing, and therefore to some extent owning, the research questions is adjudged to reduce objectivity and therefore scientific value. Meanwhile, the REF places little value on applied work.

IF POLITICS IS ARATIONAL, WHAT PRICE POLICY?

Critics of the impact category in REF 2014 rightly complain about the naivety of the models within which impact was supposed to be registered and assessed – though they might be quizzed on why social science had for so long downplayed if not ignored dissemination, co-production and the involvement of decision makers in deciding what knowledge they wanted and when. In principle, impact should see that findings and insights useful to policy makers and practitioners come from a pool of knowledge, only part of which is methodologically approved and which is deepened by practitioners themselves knowing and simultaneously doing. Defining an exclusive category of evidence for policy as coming from particular kinds of research is to misunderstand the interpenetration of belief, experience, factual knowledge, deference to authority and contingency. Heterogeneity is the name of the game (Hallsworth and Rutter, 2011). Beware misunderstanding politics and over-estimating 'the clarity of mind and singleness of purpose which any real political actor can afford for any length of time' (Dunn, 2000: x). Intellectuals, would-be suppliers of evidence for policy, may, in John Dunn's words,

> narrow the cast list of political agency recklessly to provide themselves with a manageable plot line. They mistake the rhetoric of coherence and steadiness of

purpose for the reality of improvisation, trade-offs, confusion, discomfiture and sheer fatigue. They see much too much of the relevant causality as coming from the experience and mental operations of a few individuals and much too little of it as coming from far outside this narrow space, and flooding constantly into it in ways which even the most dominant and alarming of political leaders cannot begin to prevent. (Dunn, 2000: 194)

Admonitions like that abound and have been uttered, seemingly ignored, for many years. They run the risk of declaring intellectuals (academics) and actors to be essentially different. It's an argument hard to sustain. As the evidence for policy movement peaked during the New Labour years, there was a moment of curious alignment between the neo-liberal (or neo-conservative) demand to decouple financial and fiscal decisions from politicians and hand them to experts and the (left-inflected) assertion by social science academics that, after all, they know best. In this story line a symbolic moment was granting the Bank of England operational independence, as if macroeconomics was a toolkit: give the governor a 2 per cent inflation target and to hit it he would pull the levers and push the knobs (the most obvious of which was interest rates). It turned out that tools in the kit were deficient; the plumbers did not understand how the piping worked; what they thought was money wasn't and was being created, along with vast mounds of credit, out of their sight and hearing. Debate was and remains confused. Democratic politics is suffering from a tendency to depoliticisation associated with the displacement of responsibility for policy making or implementation to independent public authorities (Hay, 2007: 57). The evidence-for-policy movement may be complicit in reducing trust in politics. If politics is seen (by academics) with 'appalled fastidiousness as a largely meaningless and remorselessly malign disorder', then social science becomes a cleanser of the Augean stables (Dunn, 2000: 355). But who does the shovelling?

A RANDOM WALK THROUGH 50 YEARS OF KNOWLEDGE

A revenant from 1965 might not be surprised at the volume of knowledge generated thanks to research council funding – that, after all, was one purpose of the creation. What would shock a Young or a Shonfield is its profligacy, variety and disconnectedness. It doesn't – can't – add up because it's so disparate and lacks unifying themes or brigades. Why, the revenant might ask, is this work being funded as opposed to that?

Take the example of the ESRC-funded Deafness Cognition and Language Research Centre (DCAL) at University College London – launched in 2006 and the largest research centre in this field in Europe (https://www.ucl.ac.uk/dcal). It has produced work on the neuroscience of sign language, early language development in deaf children, and on British Sign Language, leading to compilation of its first online dictionary. The question isn't the worth of the studies – assuming they are being read, marked and digested by signers and people with hearing loss. It's that such work might equally have been funded by the Medical Research Council or by health research or a charity. Into what strategic priority did the work fit; where is it heading? Was the decision to support the work an ad hoc response to interest on the part of academics or part of a cogent attempt to give the UK scale and capacity in the field, as part of a concerted strategy? A strategy goes beyond saying here is work of commendable interest with potential real world pay off; it says concentration of resource here (over time) is part of a knowing choice to make progress, accepting there will be ups and downs and the exact course of knowledge accumulation is unpredictable.

Our revenant would certainly be disappointed. Heyworth, a businessman from a north of England background, was well aware even in the 1960s of regional disparity: regional development was a major policy theme for the Wilson government, with its selective employment tax and decentralisation programmes. Fifty years later, it is not just that – the UK having grown – relative economic disparities have grown, but that social science knowledge no longer seems relevant. Compare the pessimistic, even fatalistic tone of Overman (2015) surveying the figures showing concentration of reward, skill and people in London, arguing that these cannot be replicated elsewhere. The prospects of regenerating many (all) of the supplicant cities of the north are dark. The evidence suggests that agglomeration economies work at smaller scales than the entire Northern economy, so more uneven development across Northern cities may be necessary if we want one of these cities to provide the kind of opportunities available in London. 'The traditional policy mix – central government investments in local growth projects, transport and other infrastructure, funding for business support and access to finance, and a host of other interventions – is largely ineffective' (Overman, 2015: 1). Our returning spirit would not criticise the studies that support this pessimistic conclusion but reflect perhaps on the impotence of 'theory' – and empirical study – in the face of big, long-run swings in capital accumulation and the absence (given such trends were glimpsed on and off from 1965 onwards) of efforts to mobilise any vital countervailing forces.

A Michael Young or his political ally Crosland would without doubt rue the distance – a gap approaching irrelevance – between the research council and performance in the public sector, the absence of any sense of mission on the part of social science to do with improvement. Hood and Dixon (2015) peer into a black hole – the lack of reliable time-series data for such basics of evaluation as spending on staff. If not the state, should the research council be ascribed any responsibility in this field as a custodian or guarantor? To pose the question is to expose it as naïve. The ESRC, conscious of its status low down the pecking order, was never likely to challenge the Whitehall system of which it was an appendage – just as (to broaden the point) the statutory bodies, the UK Statistics Authority and the NAO may occasionally complain but have mounted no thoroughgoing critique of the quality of the data necessary to evaluate public sector performance. But might the ESRC have been more directive, more strategic in trying to push research? Yes, though that again would have demanded from the research council a sense of responsibility, even ownership of the basic health of a system of which it was a lowly part.

Of course the research council has produced and curated huge mounds of social data, which would have to be part of any wider assessment of 'performance'. But how to connect them either with policy or prospects for collective – or individual – action? Take the compilation of 'findings' put together from the longitudinal and cohort studies (ESRC, 2004b). In 1965, the average 7-year-old lived with 2.1 other children. Given that just over 1 per cent of these children were living in stepfamilies, only a tiny minority of these other children would have been step-siblings. Nearly 40 years later, the average child aged between 6 and 8 lives with only 1.5 other siblings, of whom around 10 per cent are step-siblings or half-siblings. The analysts discuss such changes, with the growth in unmarried and same sex partnerships, under the heading individualisation, noting the trends vary socially and geographically. But the choices about family and living together are 'dependent on context; they are constrained by social class, the local economy and local culture'.

These trends are paralleled by declining attachment to community. These are, as it were, after the event studies, telling how people have been living social change, becoming single mothers, leaving husbands and wives, creating new households. What is missing is explanation, notably in any form that would undergird collective action – policy or changed group consciousness. The Council's founders would probably celebrate the life course studies that help identify such trends. But they might also be alarmed. Has social science been forecasting or even keeping up with the dialectic of individual choice and constraint by class, culture and economic circumstance? Why did individualisation triumph in the form of choices to decouple from cross-identification with others (community) or detachment from the means of securing collective benefits (political participation)? If social science could proffer such explanation in real time, might it feed back into the meld of choice and constraint, perhaps giving social actors a clearer sense of what they could and couldn't do, where they might resist and where they were, more or less, fated?

Andrew Shonfield had looked sceptically at comparative UK performance, macroeconomic policy, investment trends and the organisation of companies (Shonfield, 1965). On his return in 2015, what would he make of the decades of intellectual dominance, in economics as in business studies, of American versions of corporate purpose, emphasising executive leadership and fixation on short-run equity valuations? Principal agent modelling, subscription to individual choice, indifference to the institutional detail of markets – what had the research council done about this failure?

6

ACADEMIC CAPTURE

SUMMARY

The research council became a club, or mutual for academics: a mechanism for distributing support, geared to the identity of disciplines, not the 'problems' that its founders had envisaged it tackling.

'Academic capture' makes it sound conspiratorial. It's meant in Dahrendorf's sense that 'social science lost its intrinsically public character' and failed to resist the 'built-in tendency towards autarky' in which guilds and sects compete and exclude (Dahrendorf, 1995a). In parallel, the Council became – and remains – 'a fair shares cooperative' for academics (Walker, 1975b). The phrase was coined by Jeremy Mitchell, the SSRC scientific secretary from 1966, perhaps bearing in mind the Robbins' Report judgement on Oxford and Cambridge – 'syndicalist organisations, pure examples of producers' democracy' (Howson, 2011: 919). Young encountered academic self-interest within months of the SSRC's founding. 'It was clear that the first concern of the Sociology or almost any other committee was going to be the advancement of sociology rather than Heyworth's elusive "benefits"' (Young, 1975: 5). To counter this, Mitchell urged dirigisme – a French word needed to characterise an un-British bid to brigade intellectual endeavour. This – his successor, Cyril Smith, told me in an interview (Walker, 1975b) – was inevitable. If the social sciences contributed towards solving social problems, the SSRC had a part to play in 'giving some direction' to the processes involved, said Derek Robinson, who became executive chair in 1976 (SSRC, 1976: 17).

DIRIGISME

My contention would be strongly resisted by academics. They believe that over the years the Council has become more directing, insisting a larger proportion of grants fall under its rubrics. Grants were tainted, academics said, because they were awarded as reflections of the interests of dominant interests, false politicians, making the Council Whitehall cat's paw.

Claire Donovan looked in detail at the period from 1966 to the mid-1990s (Donovan, 2001); to the period since 2006 I can bring my personal experience. Her evidence is that the ESRC operated more like a clever intermediary than a transmission belt. I would add that it conducted a kind of game or semi-conscious subterfuge, signalling to Whitehall it was buying academic attention to stipulated problems (of a generalised kind) while signalling to academics that, provided they paid lip service to the rubrics, their autonomy was undisturbed. The rubrics can hardly be called intrusive. 'Themes' were allowable as long as they 'belong to nobody', especially not politicians and administrators. But for budgetary reasons (this is Ralf Dahrendorf in the 6th ESRC annual lecture) the Council has to sort of promise to contribute to the needs of users on, say, economic competitiveness or the effectiveness of public services (Dahrendorf, 1995a). But we don't know – and can never know – whether research will deliver such goods: instead we'll pretend.

Take the call for 'transformative' research. Civil servants' predilection for buzz-words and incantations grew with the advent of the 'new public management': underperforming and allegedly over-costly services were to be transformed by the application of formula, often supplied by management consultants and often involving contracting and private sector involvement. Officials of an arm's-length body would be likely to reflect back to parent department their awareness of and enthusiasm for the latest cry. This explains the ESRC call for 'genuinely transformative research ideas' (the new public management loves pleonasm as well as bathos and tautology) 'enabling research that challenges current thinking' (ESRC, 2013d). Transformative research 'would encourage novel developments of social science enquiry and support research activity that attracts an element of risk'. Of course this is bureaucrat speech. Of course any 'science' worth its name would be likely to challenge current thinking. But it's far from empty; it's speech with a purpose. It signals to BIS that the ESRC is on message, aware of ministerial and departmental fashion. As for researchers, who will be complaining about 'direction', it leaves them almost untrammelled. By the definition above anything could be 'transformative'. So money under this programme went, inter alia, to work on smartphone applications to enhance longitudinal survey methods – surely incremental and a project on 'mental life in the city' on the frontiers of sociology and neuroscience.

As for bureaucratic direction, Donovan gives an extraordinary example. The doyen of social mobility studies, one of the most highly regarded sociologists of recent times, applied to the SSRC for support for a large-scale study; but John Goldthorpe was turned down by his peers. It was only funded, after successive rejections, through the intervention of Andrew Shonfield (Donovan, 2001: 160). Was he acting on behalf of ministers (Tory at the time)? Or being suborned by a mafia of Oxford dons (as insinuated by some)? Or merely acting as a perspicacious observer of modern Britain, seeing that such a study would be tremendously interesting with potential policy relevance? It's true – an auto-biographical note – I had to struggle to get an account of the resulting work (published as Goldthorpe, 1980) into the *Economist*, sociology not being in high regard in that quarter. But the rigour of the analysis impressed even the editor of the Britain section – Sarah Hogg, now a Tory baroness, whose father-in-law (Quentin Hogg, Lord Hailsham) had played a walk-on role in setting up the Heyworth Committee. A further irony was that the Goldthorpe and Halsey social mobility studies were cited by the SSRC itself in its self-justifying submission to Rothschild (Halsey, 2004: 140).

THE SSRC TRIES TO THINK FOR ITSELF

Organisation, involving teams, virtual laboratories, research management and leadership, the founders believed, was a precondition for modern social research. Problems did not conform to disciplinary boundaries. 'The intellectual requirements of effective multi-disciplinary research are not always readily met by the existing departmental structures of universities', was Shonfield's point (Walker, 1975b). 'It may be regarded as one of the specific purposes of a research council concerning itself with the whole range of the social sciences to invent institutional means of resisting the powerful tendency towards the excessive compartmentalisation of the individual disciplines'. Academic departments were and remain congeries of individuals. 'So pleasurable is the lack of a defined division of labour that any attempt to engage in large-scale research enterprises has led to the grafting onto university structures of organisational entities in which such a division of labour is possible' (Rossi, 1964, quoted in Bulmer, 1978: 42). That early 1960s observation provided the template for successive Council efforts to combat university autarky – with programmes, initiatives, centres and the like. However, in the 1990s, an ESRC official noted that 'centres do not sit comfortably in the departmental structure', especially when it came to trans- or inter-disciplinary work (Bulmer, 1996: 90).

Young, influenced by the Medical Research Council, moved to equip the SSRC itself to do research. So entrenched has the doctrine of academic autonomy become that it now sounds almost outlandish that the Council could set up in-house research teams. Perhaps the effort was doomed. Among conditions for its success was the existence of a pool of non-academic researchers – another 'might have been' is the active promotion by the Council of a research cadre outside the universities. It existed in embryo, supplying the few social research think tanks (notably the National Institute of Social and Economic Research and Social and Community Planning Research), but academic social science was in the throes of rapid expansion. Wistfully, some hoped the universities would be pushed by professions, the jobs market and cost pressure into conceding space to non-academic research organisations (Cherns and Perry, 1976). Instead, despite financial pressure, the universities tightened their grip. The history of the NIESR is indicative (Jones, 1988). It suffered, politically, from the anti-Keynesian backlash in the 1980s and the Tories' dislike of its brand of macroeconomic forecasting. The 'might have beens' include the NIESR's prospering as a centre for thought and analysis outside academe, which might have pushed it to a position where the creation of the OBR was superfluous; instead it became a jobbing contract research unit, with uncertain focus.

The SSRC Survey Unit ended in tears, disrupted by industrial dispute and its staff uncertain about their status. For the rest, the SSRC compromised, establishing 'units' or centres in universities. The first of these was the Survey Archive, at the University of Essex, lineal ancestor of what is now the UK Data Service. The problem then, as now, was how to get academics employed by a single university to behave as if they were part of a common infrastructure, sharing and marketing their work rather than squirrelling it away for private perusal.

Focusing research on problems, the SSRC established a race relations unit (later renamed ethnic relations). The field was contested; in it there already existed the Institute of Race Relations, which took an activist line. The SSRC's appointee as director, Michael Banton, was to be a missionary, charged with getting the social science disciplines interested in the field. The aim was intellectually rigorous work that could inform policy. But the academics wanted to build their disciplines. To some there was no conflict. John Rex, later director, said: 'I believe we can do more for the people of Notting Hill or Handsworth by setting their problems within a wide context of sociological theory than we can by ad hoc strategies which may involve mock heroics but which will be doomed to failure' (Rex, 1973). But 'action research' was fashionable and methods disputed. Money and the will were missing to support a single institution; instead, the 'unit' recruited from far-flung universities in London, Manchester and Bristol. There was no overall plan. Housing was under-researched. Policy makers were not happy. The Community Relations Commission thought the unit should be taking their findings and directing them to policy issues, but the academics denied basic information existed. Ethnic relations was quickly swallowed by sociology as 'its' subject matter.

Explaining the defeat of the original version points as much to government structure and attitudes as to higher education. The Home Office had established its own in-house research unit eight years before the SSRC was created, and since then it has kept control, jealous of interventions (including the race relations unit). It maintained strong bilateral and contractual relationships with criminologists and academics working on policing. The pattern continues to this day. The recent What Works centre on policing and crime reduction is one of the least autonomous, the Home Office's College of Policing taking ownership.

DIRIGISME DEFEATED

The dirigistes were defeated. They got their themes and strategic priorities and packaging of the ostensible research interests of commerce, capitalism and the state (which some would argue are indistinguishable). But university social scientists won. Since the early 1970s, the Council has not thought hard about the conditions within which knowledge is best produced. The likes of Mitchell and Smith have not been seen since the 1970s – social science literate non-academics, with a strategic imagination. Smith, secretary of the SSRC from 1975, was a professional sociologist by background, a contemporary of Chelly Halsey at the London School of Economics, who had even been chair of the British Sociological Association. But he had also acquired government experience as director of studies for social policy and social administration at the Civil Service College. Robinson and his successor, Michael Posner, were Oxbridge dons, but integrated into political life and, in Robinson's case, the unions. I noted, after interviewing Robinson, that he is an applied economist and statistician and his political connexions made him 'a mixed blessing in the eyes of many social scientists' (Walker, 1975c).

Their successors, as we have seen, were all fully-fledged academics. More than that, the '70s saw the monopolisation of knowledge production by the universities, and with the installation of 'excellence' as its principal test the victory of epistemological monism. Research on questions of policy is needed, David Donnison wrote in the 1970s, and governments should take steps to promote such work 'because it will not be effectively or economically done if it is left entirely to universities, the research councils and research foundations' (Donnison in Bulmer, 1978: 65). A prime reason was that the research workers need to be prepared to take part in multilateral exchanges with policy makers and politicians, preferably on the back of pre-existing networks.

The Council has always been ambiguous about the independent research organisations; it was not responsible for their health or survival. Political Economic Planning died, merged into the Centre for Studies in Social Policy to become the Policy Studies Institute, which flowered then itself died (or was absorbed into a university). The Tavistock Institute is a pale shadow; the Institute of Community Studies died, ditto the Centre for Environmental Studies and the Centre for Studies in Social Policy. Social and Community Planning Research lives still as NatCen, but hand to mouth.

The Institute for Fiscal Studies, born 1969, has become the Council's poster child since its adoption in 1990; it is one of the most significant social science institutions in recent times. Not all that glisters is gold, however. Funding for the IFS has been touch and go; academic 'peers' resent its money and have lobbied, so far without complete success, to cut it adrift; its exact status along-side a kosher academic centre at University College, London is opaque. In 1990, it was the ESRC centre that was to 'take forward the pioneering work of the IFS in areas such as taxation, social security and labour supply' (ESRC, 1990). Notwithstanding the academic work of Richard Blundell, it has been the non-academics under distinguished direction (Andrew Dilnot, Robert Chote, Paul Johnson) who have had impact under these headings because it is grounded in politics and fiscal practice. When the ESRC wants to demonstrate relevance and immediacy, it is the IFS work that tends to get cited. In Britain in 2015 (ESRC, 2014b) 10 per cent of research cited with a specific URL came from the IFS; five years earlier, for comparison, the figure was 6 per cent (ESRC, 2009). Pronouncing, with rigour and data, on party manifestos, pledges and official documents, the IFS built intellectual authority (inflated, somewhat, in a political culture largely innumerate and innocent of public finance understanding). Placing the IFS in the state's knowledge architecture is intriguing when Treasury officials attend its public presentation of inferences and extrapolations from the Treasury's own spending data. The state, in the shape of the Cameron coalition, created a brand new body to comment on budget projections, the Office of Budget Responsibility – work that could have been done by an existing organisation (the IFS or contracted through the ESRC). That the latter was not considered says something about the administrative distance between the research council and the centre of the state, despite the presence on the ESRC's council of the Treasury chief economic adviser and his deputy.

Victory for the doctrine of academic autonomy created – and goes on making for – a structural problem for this publicly funded supplier of knowledge. What if academics' curiosity does not lead where policy makers, business, society want to know more; what if their interests leave yawning gaps, methodological as well as substantive?

BUT CURIOSITY LEAVES GAPS

At its birth, the SSRC struggled to align the public interest in advancing knowledge (preferably for use) with the private interest of disciplinarians. They saw the research council as a mechanism for passing them money. Early debates were about how much for sociology, whether geography should join the party and whether education deserved a board rather than a mere committee. The problems facing Britain during the late 1960s did not altogether fit; the fate of successive chiefs was to struggle to escape the iron cage. Before Robin Matthews stood down as chair he had created a 'research initiatives board' – a kind of backstop and think tank. But this implied the SSRC itself had a mind and capacity separate from the academics to whom it gave money. The very existence of the research initiatives board seemed to offend some. An early test was North Sea oil, the exploitation of which raised myriad questions across the disciplines including – if social science raised the question whatever answer it gave was ignored by the Callaghan and Thatcher governments – establishing the proceeds from taxing oil as an investment fund, rather than consuming them in paying for government's day-to-day expenses.

The SSRC established a blue ribbon advisory group to tell it whether research should be concentrated in one department with grants and studentships channelled accordingly or, as in the past, should wait for academics to come forward, showing their curiosity (or not) in aspects of the phenomenon. The panel consisted of Dudley Sears of IDS at Sussex, Gary Runciman and Sir Robert Grieve, retired professor of town and regional planning at Glasgow. What they found did not inspire confidence: work was patchy and discipline bound. But rivalries political and institutional fuelled criticism of any move to concentrate the research effort. The SSRC set up a panel to give grants. The resulting work has not been evaluated in a formal way but it is hard, in retrospect, to see its having had influence or been intellectually outstanding. Would concentration have secured those ends?

The doctrine of curiosity emphasises contingency and so gives little or no help to an organisation responsible for infrastructure and data. The problem has crystallised as the scale of investment in longitudinal data sets has grown. It's the equivalent of, what if we held a party and no one came? Expensive archives, very expensive sweeps of a cohort offer a poor investment if they are not exploited. If the UK had more 'intermediary' funders of research we would see the infrastructure better exploited, but such funders would, rightly, have questions to which they would like answers.

The ESRC has tried financial incentives – a special fund in the shape of its Secondary Data Analysis Initiative, to pay for studies of existing data. It has tried to offer the data gatherers a sweetheart deal, an easy route to their own investigation of the data they were meant to collate and disseminate as a collective resource. The doctrine says the dynamics of community will ensure that sooner or later researchers will come forward – but meanwhile someone might ask a value for money question. Is the volume of research commensurate with the cost of the data; is it productive enough? That, however, is a class of question that rarely gets asked – though one data set, the decennial census, has been subject to rigorous appraisal, even a cost benefit analysis. Another is whether plural research centres (the spread of investment in longitudinal studies, for example) produces desired intellectual competition or merely jealousy and duplication. The ESRC had tried at points to concentrate publicly funded resources and been seen off by the academics (ISER, n.d. a: 5).

By the end of the '70s, the die was cast. The Council should keep an eye 'on the "timeliness" and social purpose of the work they sponsor in the universities', but its first responsibility is 'the advancement of knowledge through good research rather than the enlightenment of debates about policy' (Bulmer, 1978: 63). The result has been constant friction and, in public spending terms, overlap and ambiguity. The Council has run initiatives, established research centres, mounted programmes, all carrying labels that suggested they answered knowledge imperatives. Some overlapped with – and secured the support of – Whitehall departments and agencies. But their involvement was usually partial, unengaged and dependent on individual civil servants' commitment (in a career structure biased against longevity and subject expertise). Government kept asking just what the social sciences – personified by the SSRC – could offer the policy maker. The passage of the years has, if anything, deepened prevalent ambiguity about the relationship of social science to decision making by political and administrative actors. Patricia Thomas of the Nuffield Foundation used the phrase 'suspension of disbelief' (Thomas, 1985: 8). Researchers claim to be influencing policy; policy makers commission research, albeit at arm's-length, but in between both what government does and social outcomes are remarkably uninflected.

The official line is that the ESRC supports the research community in pursuing curiosity driven work, allowing academics to define their own priorities – as well as research that seeks a more direct application or to address 'key global challenges'. It exists to 'serve the community' – leaving open the question (a) whether there is indeed a community of social scientists rather than a congeries of disciplines and (b) who, in turn, the community of social scientists serves. The Council has tended not to address accountability, except in the weak form of requiring grant holders to write end-of-project reports.

ACADEMIC FREEDOM – FROM WHAT?

What did for the original conception of the SSRC as a public producer of knowledge was the doctrine of academic freedom. It was often expressed defensively. As Shonfield said (using the male pronoun as people did then), it was a prevalent suspicion that 'anything which might induce a scholar to diverge by ever so little from the direction of his spontaneous choice, on the ground that the new course might result in something of practical use, distorted the undertaking completely' (Shonfield, 1972b: 427). He believed – a common understanding at the time – that social science research had to be managed, planned for. 'Academic individualism ... cannot provide the basic criterion on which the organisations necessary for the development of the social sciences can be built. It can play the role only of a subordinate part' (Trist, 1972: 131).

Andrew Shonfield is the SSRC's tragic figure. The Clapham Committee had feared 'the best men' being diverted from doing research to coordinating research. Shonfield recognised and exemplified the falsity of this: research organisation and administration should be sites of excellence. But the universities would not tolerate Erastian social science. Shonfield shared and deepened Michael Young's vision of social science as policy science, yet it was during his tenure as executive chair that the SSRC started definitively to become and, as it turned out, inescapably a mechanism for funding disciplinary research while government itself went its own way, creating a social science research function alongside and, usually, indifferent to the SSRC. Nearly 40 years after its foundation, the Blunkett question remained apposite, asking why so much social science appeared 'supplier driven'.

At its strongest, the doctrine said academics were perfectly capable of deciding on what might result in something of practical use – deciding they did not like it and refusing to do it (but continuing to be supported by public funds). This underpins the extraordinary procedure in the REF through which academics judge their own 'impact'. Commissioned research – some academics would extend the point to cover guided or 'strategic' research – becomes little more than 'a public relations tool' (Hammersley, 2002: 33). The line of thinking goes like this. Making academics accountable undermines trust in their professional judgement – a professionalism that requires no formal certification or membership dues, except the now prevalent assumption that they possess a doctoral degree. Academic research is a different order of knowledge creation from research that may be done by practitioners or governments. We and they live in different worlds with distinctive orientations. We offer enlightenment, not engineering. Hammersley is unspecific about who is enlightened and how, claiming it has to do with inform-ing public debate – which would imply academics are seen and heard in a wider domain than peer-reviewed journals.

The dirigistes – inhabiting the world of ministers, budgets, media, parties and opinion – were unconvinced that the instincts of university professors were infallible guides to what matters. They asserted that the Council had a right and duty to inspect what academics were doing within their disciplines. Shonfield wanted the SSRC to have 'influence on the development of certain of the social sciences' (Shonfield, 1972b: 428). At its gentlest, this might have been a bid to ask, 'why so much focus on x, why not pay more attention to y?', where x might be poverty and y might be a burgeoning class of wealthy, apparently able to escape tax while influencing politics and policy.

TRAJECTORIES OF DISCIPLINES

What if (as happened) a discipline went awry? Economics started to lose touch with the institutional and behavioural reality of markets and misunder-stand or ignore an entire sector of the economy (finance). 'In no other field of empirical inquiry has so massive and sophisticated a statistical machinery been used with such indifferent results', said Wassily Leontief, one of the dis-cipline's own as long ago as 1971 (quoted in Nathan, 1988: 31), 'Continued preoccupation with imaginary, hypothetical rather than observable reality has led to a distortion of the valuation scale used in our academic commu-nity to assess and to rank the performance of its members'. Yet economics, as a set of tools and a means of framing questions to make them manageable, was always going to appeal to policy makers. At issue is whether the Council could ever have interpolated inside the discipline, separating the transient from enduring qualities.

Meanwhile, what if sociology disappeared down the rabbit hole and aban-doned any study of economic behaviour and institutions? Did the research funders have no say? What became clear before the SSRC's first decade was out was that at least one discipline – university sociology – had gone AWOL. Paul Barker, editor of *New Society*, talked about a feeling that 'far too much sociology is devoted to class (though race risks running it close) as if it were the be-all subject' (Barker, 1972: 12). But he was not an academic; such views could be dismissed (and were) as philistine or merely rightwing. Something had unquestionably gone wrong. One naturally expects – an unhappy 1970s sociologist observed:

to find a significant proportion of them busily engaged in prosecuting longitudinal inquiries, panel studies, twin studies, controlled trials, double-blind experiments, rating studies, instrumentation exercises and calibration studies … In fact they are doing none of these. With few exceptions they are lecturing, writing books about books, engaging in journalism and talking about the thesis they never quite finished or the bit of participant observation that they may do one day. (Hope, 1978: 262)

I attended the 1975 conference of the British Sociological Association, still registered for my PhD at the University of Sussex. There I had sat through seminars where self-styled ethnomethodologists had attempted to reject the entire apparatus of external (i.e. research-based) understanding. ('Bizarre' and 'absurd' are among Chelly Halsey's adjectives; Halsey, 2004: 134.) Sociology, as Ralf Dahrendorf later told the conference, seemed to have lost interest in power and become preoccupied with the underdog and subjectivity. Sociologists embraced 'inconsistent beliefs in the possibility of turning the world upside-down in order to make the unofficial official and the subterranean world the place to live (Dahrendorf, 1995a). The point isn't whether Dahrendorf was right in his characterisation, but whether the principal public funder of sociological research (the SSRC) had any response to the criticism. A related point had been made years before. 'By fixing attention upon variables about which no action can be taken most sociologists provide theoretical and explanatory structures that have neither interest nor promise for the social problem-solver because he cannot use them as handles or levers' (Riecken, 1969).

Under the strict terms of the doctrine of peer review, the Council might be allowed to pay for a review of a discipline, but what was unclear was what might happen if the review found gaps or problems of quality. Though recent peer reviews of sociology and politics have found them to be world-class, it's hard to escape a sense these social science disciplines have been mugged by reality. Why we know so little about high-income groups is a pertinent question *now* but was put, in just those terms, by Frank Bechhofer in the early 1970s (Barker, 1972). Yet in 2015 bright young sociologists would be urging their colleagues to 'wake up to the problems of the super rich' (Davies, 2015). Neither discipline nor research funder had been able, assuming they had been aware, to redirect intellectual effort towards a phenomenon that during the past decade and a half has reshaped much of London, instituted a kind of plutocracy in the governance of the UK, contributed mightily to the financial crash and weighed on indices of equality.

Occasionally lay people, practitioners and users are let in and then, if they can muster the audacity, they write on the grant applications: 'I do not dispute the value of their method in itself, but if it is meant to throw light on the problem the applicant says he wishes to illuminate, I can only say that it cannot possibly do so' (Eversley, 1978: 299). They tend not to be invited back.

At its foundation, the Council was aware of disciplinary deformations. One of the most glaring was quantitative skills. It remains so. The ESRC invests in data that too many social scientists cannot begin to handle. 'The culture of UK sociology tends to reject the view that systematic population data and statistical methods to analyse such data deserve a central place in education, training and in research' (BSA, HaPs, ESRC, 2010). A good ethnographer – a good sociologist – should also be able to handle statistics and understand the principles of sample surveying; UK social science disciplines have too often said to themselves either/or. Successive inquiries find students graduating in and postgraduates pursuing dissertations in social science without adequate methodological and statistical skills, especially in sociology, politics and nearby fields; the picture in economics and psychology is different. In the face of the disciplines' inertia – and outright resistance – the Council has been impotent.

7

CUMULATIVE KNOWLEDGE?

SUMMARY

The official claim is that 50 years of research council spending has advanced knowledge and deepened understanding – look at the volume of output and expansion of the enterprise. But evidence of 'cumulation' is sketchy. Much social science knowledge is context and institution bound; it is non-linear. What relationship, if any, obtains between the onrush of knowledge and outcomes in economy and society? Deep knowledge appears to have little or no capacity to change belief.

If academics did 'take over', did they succeed in advancing social science? The official answer is self-evidently positive. 'There is far deeper insight into economic issues than was possible 50 years ago', says Sir Christopher Pissarides (Ince, 2015). Social scientists (when they think about it, which isn't often) take it for granted that knowledge is cumulative, that factual questions admit solutions and we can continually advance our understanding. This is of course positivism – a label many social scientists would run a mile from.

Superficially, the positivists have it. Over a half-century the business of academic social science has grown hugely. Measuring growth by university positions, numbers of journals, articles published, conferences attended, the expansion is phenomenal. But this is the clutter of knowledge. Judging the intellectual bite of social science would require evaluations of constituent disciplines. There are few if any generic social scientists. The bones of knowledge as displayed by the curators of research excellence are economics, psychology, geography, and so on. Again, it's self-evident that in 2015 there is more sociology and a greater volume of business studies. But does that imply the successful PhD candidate of today or professor in one of the disciplines stands head and shoulders above their forerunners of 1965, giants on the shoulders of dwarves? What might constitute progress? That they deploy more theory, can number in their armoury more tested and unchallenged causal propositions, can predict social action better having knowledge of prior conditions? When in a half-century round-up of his discipline, Pissarides says: 'we all know people will cheat if they can get away with it' (therefore we should blame regulators, not economists, for failing to anticipate the 2008 crash), he is rewriting economics' willingness to entertain sociological concepts (cheating), the massive institutional nexus within which such concepts have any meaning (policing, disapproval, moral rearmament) and the principal models and intellectual structures through which economics research has actually operated. In the same article, Paul Johnson of the IFS says tools, data and methods have improved; he makes a quantitative elision: as the number of economists has grown, so has the 'nation's capacity to produce econometric analyses' (Ince, 2015). This, we have to assume, is irony.

Physicists and technologists tell stories about deep – 'fundamental' – inquiry conducted in obscure laboratories that years later emerges into the light to be adopted and adapted (often with the unacknowledged support of the state), becoming phones and weapons system and adding to the equity value of Vodaphone and Racal. Social science isn't like that, and not just in terms of profitability. How far does research 'cumulate', either by moving down a pathway between basic and applied or by acquiring value in the passage of time? Few social scientists are as open as David Hargreaves, who openly admits that education (sociology) simply lacks cumulative evidence (Hargreaves, 1996).

Social science's problems in claiming progress are many, even before we consider how those claims might be judged by policy makers, practitioners and the public. Claus Moser said that social science measures applied to a particular context of place, time and circumstance (Nicol, 2001: iii): they have to be historicist. So much knowledge turns out to be contextual, to depend on a given set of institutions. It cannot be applied later (i.e. now) or in different circumstances. It is light in terms of a supra-historical or general theory of social action or behaviour. Does that mean it's just one damn thing after another or – as sociological prophets of relativism might put it, falling avidly on the work of Thomas Kuhn – successive paradigms, each as valid as the next?

The ESRC website doesn't display work paid for years ago: there is not much by way of corporate memory. Grant getters are not required to scan existing literature; synthesis wins no brownie points in research assessment exercises. The effort to winnow, to package, even to conduct systematic reviews has been sporadic and under-resourced, but occasionally brilliant – for example

ESRC (2004b). In 1998 the ESRC launched Regard as a database on previous research awards. It had a brief life. Academics, generally, are more interested in new awards, new grants. The public was not able to make much sense of raw research reports; they will always need filtering and interpretation.

THE QUEEN'S QUESTION TO THE ECONOMISTS

Take migration, a phenomenon of huge contemporary significance. An ESRC funded Norface project using data from the Netherlands and other countries from 1999–2007 is reported as showing 'that labour migrants leave quickly if they are out of employment, regardless of whether they came to the country from old or new EU members' (ISER, n.d. a). Leave aside quibbles, such as the normative nature of judgements around speed of exit. This can only be a finding specific to one set of policies and institutions. How far can it generalise to, say, the UK 2008–15 or Germany 2012–20, where – because of different patterns of previous migration, social networking and geographical concentration – migrant workers might be more likely to stay if economic conjuncture turned sour. Is the finding robust enough to support a policy proposition to governments, along the lines of: admit workers from Eastern Europe, safe in the knowledge that if unemployment rises they will leave, lessening the prospect of social unrest and political challenge from anti-migration parties?

By what factor was knowledge about the macroeconomy in the first decade of the SSRC less than now? A related question has to be: even if economists' understanding of certain variables had improved (because of more sophisticated modelling or better measurement), does it have any more circulation among the public or decision makers? These are far from straightforward queries. Economics has ideological trappings; macroeconomists disagree on fundamentals (national debt, money, credit); chancellors operate by hunch and rule of thumb as well as by reference to Treasury or academic modelling. Historians might compare the chancellor in the Heath government, Tony Barber, with George Osborne, or Roy Jenkins (chancellor from 1968 to the end of the Wilson government) with Gordon Brown. They might conclude, perfectly reasonably, that the earlier politicians were judicious or perspicacious, error prone or unlucky. They would be unlikely to say Jenkins and Barber operated in a cloud of unknowing and misunderstanding any denser than that surrounding Brown and Osborne – though what they did not know about what they misunderstood were different. Whatever Jenkins or Barber did not know, we have not yet found ways of attaining a steady rate of growth with full employment and without inflation; nor have

satisfactory improvements in Britain's relative productivity performance yet
been achieved. How far, if at all, was Barber's relationship with Leslie O'Brien,
then governor of the un-independent Bank of England, less inflected by
prevalent (research-derived) knowledge than Osborne's with Mark Carney?

Appropriate metaphors here do not seem to be dwarves on giants' shoulders or bricks laid upon bricks. Remember Michael Young's hope that social
science knowledge would allow more control. In economics more knowledge
has been correlated with the triumph of the belief that in markets lack of control is not only good but necessary. The effect of tax and spend decisions can
now be modelled in advance. But not predicted. At what rate of income tax do
corporate executives work less hard (and would a marginal reduction in their
efforts affect corporate profitability, let alone aggregate growth)? At what rate
of benefit withdrawal do poor households resort to foodbanks? Some economists would answer confidently; the honest ones would be diffident. At what
ratio of public debt to GDP does the rate of economic growth reduce? Some
economists confidently answered, but it turned out their data was dodgy and
their results biased.

Staying with economics, we might ask whether 50 years of public investment in research excellence has reduced the discipline's ideological content,
that is to say, the temptation some economists cannot refuse to substitute
ought for is to align private and corporate interests in their calculus of welfare.
Less pejoratively, the ESRC chair posed this question (Stewart, 2010). His own
30 years in banking ended in 2008, he said, citing time spent at Ulster Bank,
Citi Group and Goldman Sachs (he was appointed just before a banking background became a signifier of incompetence and potential malfeasance). 'One
would never have thought that one day all three would be on public support'.
But does 'one' include professional economists supported by Council grants?
Yes, Alan Gillespie (2010) said, they missed something. Economics was too preoccupied with modelling complexity to see through complexity to some basic
motives and relationships – greed, graft, tribalism. Perhaps that was a matter
of motes and beams – economics is intensely tribal. Should an indebted government cut spending in a recession? This was central to UK politics in 2010.
In the run-up to the election that year the ESRC produced a sketch of research
findings; neither they nor it answered the question.

ESRC chief executive Ian Diamond said collapse and recession created an
'urgent need for research and knowledge' (Vaitilingam, 2010). Social scientists, he said, would not have to start from scratch because social science had
addressed past recessions. But why, it might be countered, hadn't the study of
past recessions produced formulae or, more loosely, narratives through which

the build-up to a forthcoming recession might have been identified – say around 2006? The answer is that while some generalisations can be extracted from the study of past recessions there remains a large idiographic element.

The past half-century in economics could hardly be called linear. At the birth of the SSRC Keynesians appeared to be ascendant, then were outmanoeuvred and discredited by monetarists and Hayekians. Had they been in hiding or was there a mass conversion to match Peter Jay's discovery of monetarism in 1976? The Council never seemed to grapple with these 'meta' arguments about disciplinary identity … sociology going to wrack and ruin, economics being taken over by determined campaigners for market liberalism (Burgin, 2012). If economics had been in thrall to ideology (Desai, 2015), why was that tolerated, or at least not challenged in grants or proactive research calls? The research council was not, it seems, able to transcend fashion. Meghnad Desai blames it on unrealistic macro modelling trying to describe the functioning of developed economies while ignoring the financial sector and the risks blossoming inside it – Desai's own judgement may be illuminated by his joining fellow economists in signing a letter in 2010 pressing politicians to embark on a programme of stringent austerity.

Should the research council have behaved like a police officer at an accident, redirecting traffic round the car crash (traditional microeconomics) down new avenues such as behavioural economics? It's an unfair question if the Council is obliged to sit and wait for grant applications to come in; only once they do, it can join the party. If they don't, it has no standing or leverage inside the disciplines. Behavioural economics swept into the mainstream, contradicting the precepts of and models based on the previously dominant axioms of rational choice (Lunn, 2014). Induction from observed economic activity made economics both more interesting and less authoritative. In the UK government, the behavioural approach acquired heavyweight champions at the centre of power and the Council fell in line. Arguably, it might have deployed social science to fill the holes left by advocates of the behavioural approach – how much choice could consumers realistically handle (when it came to energy tariff switching, very little)? What about public understanding of data or numbers or risk (all low)?

WHAT IF KNOWLEDGE DEPENDS ON POLICY?

Knowledge depends on policy. Social scientists won't like such a bald declaration but it's an empirical observation. Take the social science of the third sector. The Council did not anticipate New Labour's enthusiasm for the third sector. Once the policy initiatives were under way, the ESRC sought collaboration with the Cabinet

Office and charities and launched the Third Sector Research Centre (TSRC). I was involved in selecting the winning bid. However, it took time (universities can be elephantine) before the TSRC started producing academic articles and working papers. By then the wagon had moved on and Cameron's short-lived enthusiasm for Big Society dominated debate. Much academic ink was spilled on conceptualising and trying to measure 'civil society', only for voluntary bodies to prove both protean (the spontaneous creation across the country of food banks was remarkable) and weak, when confronted by recession and an antagonistic government unafraid to exploit divisions and the sector's pretence that it was above or outside partisan policy making. The upshot, now, is little that could be described as enduring 'basic' knowledge about the sector but much specific to the institutional set up of a particular time and place in the policy cycle. The TSRC produced much of interest, but 'historical', now anachronistic. Social science that gets close to institutions loses its generality. It becomes dependent on policy, subject to the vagaries of elections, ministers and politics.

Work by the TSRC said – on the basis of backward-looking empirical study – that state funding did not 'crowd out' voluntary effort; state initiatives in social policy were often synergetic with charitable enterprise. Studies confirmed the finding of the government's own social surveys that a 'civic core' of active people carried a disproportionate share of volunteering. The trouble was, the government elected in 2010 – midway through the TSRC's life – acted as if such 'evidence' did not exist. State funding would be withdrawn, especially grants from local government and – so said the ministers in the coalition government – voluntary effort would flourish. In this sense social science fell foul of history. David Cameron and colleagues (including the Liberal Democrats) dismantled much of the apparatus of support for the third sector created by Labour and turned the Charity Commission into an instrument of vengeance against charities daring to trespass into politics and campaigning. At the end of the project, the ESRC said civil society in the UK would be stronger as a result of this investment despite the project having confronted 'complex and challenging times for research on policy and practice' in the sector (Boyle, n.d.). That was a diplomatic way of saying that the context of policy and practice had changed in a big way after 2010. Would the knowledge gained in the favourable era last into the unfavourable? There is every reason to doubt it.

One crude anniversary question is: in what way do we know more now than then and, assuming we do, what difference does the extra knowledge make? The second question extends well beyond the notional responsibility of a research council, touching on what decision makers know and their exposure to and use of 'research'.

BELIEF IMPERVIOUS TO KNOWLEDGE

In 1965 the UK was still in the throes of egalitarianism, despite the 13 years of Tory rule that ended the previous year. The conventional measure of income inequality was just dipping below 0.25 before rising, then plunging during the 1970s to the point of maximal equality in recent times. It then rose to today's level, in the region of 0.33, down slightly from 2008's peak. After 50 years of social science research, the UK is definitively a more unequal society.

Of course there's no causal relationship. But some correlation is not fatuous if – which is certainly the case – large amounts of social science time and effort have gone into the study of inequality and poverty, in which the Council has played a role. Indeed, as we saw in Chapter 3, the study of poverty under its aegis may have been a factor in the attempt to kill it off.

The question is whether all social science does is keep taking snapshots of the same phenomenon or whether the snapshots are each of something different. 'Mounted units boost public trust in policing' was the headline on a report of ESRC-funded work (ESRC, 2015b): not in St Peter's Fields in 1819 they didn't. The sociology of occupations 'had made progress': we know more about miners and distant water fishermen. That was in 1972 (Barker, 1972). There are precious few of either these days. The value of the snapshots depends on contemporary political and policy circumstances: miners determined political fates in 1972. Take innovation, research and industrial policy. A high-grade discussion (such as Carter, 1981) is not conceptually or empirically 'less' than contemporary debate, just different – not least in discussing long gone public bodies such as the National Enterprise Board.

DISCONNECT

The point was made eloquently by a social scientist with intense experience both as an academic and practitioner, David Eversley, former chief planner for the Greater London Council. He cited wise-after-the-event studies on variables in the physical framework of housing and places – backyard, balconies, fresh air and so on (Eversley, 1978: 283). Then there are social and economic relationships, including kinship, child-rearing practices, employment. Important, fascinating studies had been done, ethnographies of Bethnal Green, Sunderland shipyard craftsmen, service family accommodation in Germany, Shotts miners, Sparkbrook Irish, inner city immigrants … but none of the studies seemed to touch another; none of the subjects interacted with their neighbours, or their environment in a similar (generalisable) way.

Social inquiry (much of it conducted by the state directly through the statistics agencies) produced deep knowledge. But it made little or no difference to strongly held beliefs about the nature of poverty. Using, among other data sets, the British Household Panel Survey (one of the jewels in the research council crown), John Hills affirms that families dip in and out of poverty: it is not a fate or permanent condition. Here is an intriguing counterfactual. Had John Hills been older and the data available, might his analysis have been able to convince Sir Keith Joseph that poverty was not inherited and passed through the generations like a genetic stain? Hills and colleagues were not able to convince politicians of their own era, notably the Communities Secretary Eric Pickles. His 'troubled families' are the ideological descendants of Joseph's over-breeders: a lumpen or core group who (overseen by that scourge of indigence, Louise Casey) had to be pushed or prodded out of their immiserating circumstances. What had social science been doing such that Pickles could appear in the *Daily Mail* in June 2012 (Seabrook, 2013: 32) saying 'these folks are troubled, they're troubling themselves, they're troubling the neighbourhood. We need to do something about it.'

The work of Peter Townsend, credited by many with helping the 'rediscovery' of poverty towards the end of the 1960s, established or re-established the idea of relative poverty. The notion can be illustrated by surveying the lives of poor people and/or by establishing from the haves what they think is a minimum standard. Which is what Stewart Lansley and Joanna Mack did a decade on from Townsend's book and then again 20 years after that. This is good social investigation but methodologically and conceptually it shows consistency, not change (Lansley and Mack, 2015). The Council has paid for mountains of investigation and several programmes: one example among several is the Poverty and Social Exclusion project from 2012. Repetition is inescapable. What constitutes an acceptable minimum must change over time. What doesn't change much is the conclusion that the UK's economic model 'is incapable of delivering a decent minimum standard of living. It is the model that is wrong not the citizens' (Lansley and Mack, 2015: xvi). Social science expands; the unchangeability of the UK's fiscal foundations grows.

What hasn't changed, either, during 50 years, is the non-acceptance of what to social investigators may seem self-evident. In 1989 the Tory Social Security Secretary John Moore rejected the Townsend definition above. The relative definition means that, however rich a society, it will drag the incubus of poverty with it up the income scale: the poverty lobby would in their definition find poverty in paradise. A successor to Moore, Iain Duncan Smith, Secretary for Work and Pensions in the Cameron government, says the same, rejecting the conventional definition of poverty as falling below a proportion of median income, preferring a morally-coloured definition bringing in family performance in terms of job seeking, children's schooling, quality of parenting and so on. A majority broadly share Duncan Smith's atavistic views of the poor. Reality (public attitudes, policy decisions, benefit systems) rebuts the findings of social inquiry.

Social science says Britain has built a high propensity to poverty into its economic and political system since the late 1970s, linked to increasingly unequal division of power, opportunity and reward. Politicians and public attitudes say the welfare state is bloated, supports 'skivers' and needs cutting back. Townsend's social science was thus of time and place, with little or no enduring influence (on public policy). Here was the Cameron coalition reviving 'discredited theories' from the 1960s and 1970s on problem families and transmitted deprivation, 'all of whose inadequacies Townsend (1979) had discussed' (Harloe, n.d.). But were these revivals or had the Tories together with large numbers of citizens at large never shed their beliefs? Michael Harloe says Townsend 'as an active agent in society cannot be ignored or undervalued', but then adds: 'perhaps the 21st century needs another study for the times we now live in'. There, encapsulated, is the fate of much social science. It's Groundhog Day.

DOES IT MAKE A DIFFERENCE?

The Council has been a major curator, collector and disseminator of the data on which social science – at least some social science – depends. Contemplating what is now the UK Data Service, the great cohort and longitudinal studies, the material on successive elections, the visits and revisits to the workplace, it is a treasure trove. But a trove with certain characteristics. One was that potential miners often ignored it. Another was that this trove existed alongside and in no obvious relationship with several others.

In 1974 I visited the SSRC Survey Archive. Looking back at my notes and resulting article, I am struck by how many of the issues then apparent have remained open in the years since: lack of coordination among suppliers of data, especially the central government; relatively low take-up of data opportunities by academic researchers; unresolved concerns about the use (users had a worryingly 'low profile'), for research, of personal data, even anonymised. I recorded the archivists complaining of academics' 'reluctance' to deposit; later the research council required deposit as a condition of its grants. A National Council for the Data Bank was sketched, to involve government and commercial gatherers of survey material; 40 years later the absence of cross-sectoral and strategic bodies for data is notable. The significance, then, of the willing-ness of the polling company Gallup to deposit data is lessened by the absence of any plan to ensure it would be exploited. But there's no doubt about the excitement, for example collecting 'non-standard data sets' such as the surveys of east London conducted by Wilmott and Young; but no one came to study them (and find their flaws and peculiarities) for years.

One class of data invested in heavily over the half-century is also one of the most ambiguous – on polling, voting and elections. The terrain is shared with commercial firms, media and political parties themselves, which generate large amounts of data. The Council supported the British Election Study, both as a data set and ongoing analysis. The boundary between academic analysis and media reporting of politics is sometimes indistinct, studies often relying on political journalism. To public and media, election studies are a superior kind of polling analysis, but as prone to making fallible predictions. In a review of his field, John Curtice pronounced the study of British electoral behaviour to be both productive and lively; the election study series is the longest running academic survey series in Great Britain and compares favourably with election studies elsewhere in the range of information collected, even if it had been dependent, both methodologically and conceptually, upon ideas imported from elsewhere, most notably the United States (Curtice, 2002). But with what behavioural or indeed attitudinal consequences? Take voting in the UK 2010–15. You would have to look hard for signs that election studies both previous and contemporary affected the behaviour of voters in general elections, in vot-ing for police and crime commissioners, in rejecting proportional representation for the House of Commons. If election studies subsequently explained, say, the rise of the UK Independence Party or the success of the Scottish Nationalists, they failed to anticipate the rejection of a regional assembly in the North East of England (widely tipped by academic political scientists as likely). If not pre-diction, shouldn't explanatory social science have through its understanding of past action the capacity to influence and change today's or tomorrow's?

SCHOOLING MAKES LITTLE DIFFERENCE

A research council for social science was from the start supposed to expand knowledge of and for schools, students and teachers. For some, it was second best to the creation of an education research council and, at first, the SSRC gave its education research function the status of a 'board' in recognition of its salience. A half-century on, knowledge has self-evidently expanded, but identi-fying its role in education policy or student attainment is not easy. That is partly because education research has never had a strategy; the division of labour between various knowledge producing organisations has never been specified. The research council has often been marginal, certainly never a master of the field or even principal strategist.

At the inception, social science was going to provide answers. The commissioning of the Plowden Report exuded confidence in social science (Silver and Silver, 1992). The educational priority areas took its recommendations for better teachers, extra support and allowances and social work in schools and focused them on specific areas, offering 'positive discrimination', while carrying out in situ evaluation. Results were inconclusive, showing that extra resources do make a difference, without supplying a calculus of value for money.

By the late 1960s, the UK was importing American pessimism about how schools and teachers could, if at all, change the fortunes of disadvantaged young people. Alan Little judged most interventions ineffective, including the EPA. 'We are ignorant about meeting these problems [of prolonged underprivilege] within the orbit of the educational system … the lesson learned should be one of educational modesty' (Barker, 1972: 119). Is that any less true now, give or take the modesty of educational researchers? The 'London effect' – a causal proposition that spending and coordination improved results – has been downgraded, in favour of a proposition about the homes and parental aspirations of ethnic minority and migrant families (Burgess, 2014). Knowing then of the 'limited impact of schooling and school resources compared with extra-school factors', should the SSRC have given up and moved on?

In the late 1990s, just as Labour came to power, the then Department for Education and Employment calculated that £70 million a year was being spent on research commissioned, by it, together with the ESRC, the Teacher Training Agency and as part of support for university education departments by the Higher Education Funding Council for England. How much was 'useful'; how much reached classroom teachers and their students? The quality of evidence in education has not been great, with evaluations to assess the quality of interventions 'often poor' (JRF, 2014: 30). In education, social science could hardly bring itself to speak the most uncomfortable of truths to teachers, ministers of education, school inspectors and parents. The system prized the individual, passing examinations and attaining advancement; this could just about be read at the level of a school, in the form of league tables and a rhetoric of failure and success. Social science said of education – as with poverty – the phenomena are 'structural', explained by dynamics in the economy, income, and households. By implication schools matter less; what teachers can do is inherently limited; the fate of pupils is probabilistically foretold.

As early as the first decade of the SSRC, social scientists often reluctantly came to conclude that school mattered a lot less than background. Inequalities in outcomes were caused by families' resources. An obvious inference for policy makers is that helping families earn more or get more benefits would be more effective than extra spending on schooling. It's been a result resisted by policy makers in successive governments, Labour as well as Tory. Race and gender matter but in educational attainment socio-economic differences are far greater.

Education has had an up and down relationship with evidence. A large trend in national policy since the 1980s has been giving parents more choice and increasing school autonomy. They have been claimed to improve the attainment of children from poor backgrounds. There is no evidence. Pupils do better or worse because of their individual teacher, and variability between teachers is more powerful than between schools. Policy talks about 'weeding out', less about paying teachers more. To remedy or diminish disadvantage research has proven various negatives – the specific content of the curriculum makes little difference.

The pattern in education, in poverty, in economics is one in which knowledge is added to but does not necessarily 'cumulate' or lend itself to formulae for application across time and space. Knowledge generated by social science supported by the research council competes, often unsuccessfully, with knowledge generated by other forms of inquiry and consultation (and consultancy); it is unable to enforce an epistemological hierarchy or filter. Research turns out to be (at best) only one of the contributors to policy formation; common sense and 'ordinary' knowledge prove resilient. Much is idiographic, contextual, specific to time and place and institutional fate. High initial hopes that knowledge would punch through to enlightened policy (and civic improvement) are dashed. Atavistic and 'unenlightened' attitudes persist and may even strengthen. Yet disappointment is muted.

The pattern holds, more or less, for the broad field of city, urban and community studies undertaken by the research council together with regional and industrial policy. Like education, social science brought bad news to the planners, councillors and urban developers: 'structural' forces are strong, and likely to overwhelm local regeneration efforts. New studies are done, but basic problems remain. A 'brief' in *New Society* published at the time of the Thatcher government's burst of enthusiasm for urban policy (largely thanks to Michael Heseltine) complained that we had umpteen community studies without 'community' ever being satisfactorily defined; they lacked any underlying theoretical link (New Society, 1984). Development happens; regions change; but uninflected by research or indeed policy. Take East Anglia and the effect of Cambridge and 'silicon fen':

> While particular and historic government policies have played some role in the region's industrial development, most notably the decentralisation and over-spill programme of the 1960s and 1970s, East Anglia's industrial development generally owes little to policy initiatives. [It is] a case study in restructuring by powerful economic forces operating globally and within the UK's capitalist system. (Keeble, 1998: 38)

UNIMPROVED PUBLIC MANAGEMENT

A stark question: has public management improved because of research? The beginnings of an answer might note how, under the aegis of the research council, knowledge has been segmented and sequestered. Communities, including both (thinking) practitioners and (practically-minded) researchers, have disappeared. The practitioners of government don't do much thinking and the researchers speak to themselves inside protected and exclusive spaces.

With research relevant to government, what shows through is randomness. Programmes and inquiries may be interesting – which is why academics conduct them – but have no immanent relationship to what ministers, councillors and officials are doing or are likely to do. The other observation is about distance. A case study of how an unnamed city council is coping with the cuts written in an academic journal is both context-bound but also unavailable in context, as a potential guide to action by the actors studied. 'To protect the anonymity of the city in question, at an acutely sensitive time, we cannot provide extensive contextual details' (Lowndes and McCaughie, 2013: 535). Perhaps being interviewed for an academic study had therapeutic value for participants, prompting self-reflection. But they might have wondered whether their time had been cost-effectively spent on learning that they are data serving 'to generate theoretical propositions for further investigation'. Despite that, much of this kind of research has a vaguely imprecatory, even evangelical flavour, except that the preaching is confined to the covers of peer-reviewed journals.

The ESRC contributed to studies on crime, policing, student attainment, some of which were ambiguous. Smaller classes are not associated with pupil attainment; police numbers have no relationship with crime reduction. But teachers prefer smaller classes and the public likes seeing bobbies on the beat, which are also 'outcomes'. When eminent political scientists (grant aided by the ESRC) came to appraise policies that did not work, their principal observation was that ministers and officials should 'deliberate' more (King and Crewe, 2013). But the propensity to deliberate may have reduced during the past half-century, mitigating any increase in the evidence and analysis from social science that might be deployed if time for deliberation were found.

Boundaries are not impermeable, however, notably in the outlying areas of social science such as business and management. Barry Quirk, former chief executive of the London Borough of Lewisham, addressed performance by local authorities in the face of spending cuts unaccompanied by reductions in expectations or need (Quirk, 2015). Quirk, it should be noted, is exceptional: a PhD, he is an author and practitioner-thinker. His citations include government papers, specialist journalism (*Public Finance* magazine), American management literature, which itself criss-crosses boundaries between consultancy, academic research and case-study-based observations on organisational success. The ESRC supports another of his references, the IFS; he mentions work by Scott Lavery of Sheffield University working in the Political Economic Research Institute, with ESRC connections. Another, Robert Chia of Strathclyde University, was an ESRC fellow at the University of Lancaster. Professor Christopher Hood has had extensive ESRC support and led projects. Bob Garratt, a consultant and visiting professor at Cass Business School, has taken part in ESRC sponsored seminars on corporate governance. Another reference is to books by Michael Barber, the former Institute of Education professor become policy adviser, whose career interweaves with projects supported by the ESRC.

The upshot is that the way knowledge is categorised by the ESRC and academics has little or no resonance, even with thinking practitioners. What grips them is a 'problem' thrown up by their day-to-day experience, sharpened by a probably permanent sense of organisational under-performance. What they seek is knowledge to address the problem, wherever it may come from. They grade it for its perspicuity, relevance and applicability. Another conclusion is that over the years researchers dip in and out. They are usually promiscuous about sources of funding, focusing instead on their declared intellectual interests. Another point is that the ESRC often does not secure recognition for its below-the-line or infrastructural supports, for seminars, gatherings, occasions of interchange, which may sometimes involve practitioners and, what Bob Garratt calls himself, 'pracademics'.

Mentioned above is the Blair 'delivery' specialist Michael Barber, who since leaving government has been selling advice to governments. He wrote up an account of the Prime Minister's Delivery Unit and precepts based on its work (Barber, 2015). He refers to academic work, some articles in peer-reviewed journals, but does not accord it priority or 'fundamental' status: it is in a mix along with reflections on personal experience, analysis by practitioners, think tank reports. His work is not predictive but, like management consultants do, he offers models and schemes at a certain level of abstraction, into which a client might fit its version of deliverology. Barber, himself a former academic, acknowledges opportunities to lecture and interact with students and academics, including business schools at Oxford and Cambridge, the LSE and Queen Mary University London. The ESRC itself is not referenced.

8

CONCLUSION

SUMMARY

Heyworth said in 1965 that setting up the research council would be repaid by improvements in the efficiency of the national economy and quality of life. But the evidence on inequality, say, or trust in government is not compelling: it is not clear either that social science has had meliorative effects on them. Social science research has produced useful ideas with an increasingly factual base rather than definitive answers to major policy questions.

The Wilson government is convinced, Lord Snow – parliamentary secretary in the Ministry of Technology – told his fellow peers, that 'the additional expenditure by Government that we recommend' in establishing the SSRC 'will in the course of time – and not too long a time – be more than repaid by the improvement in the efficiency of the national economy' (Snow, 1965). Importantly, the Heyworth Committee had added '... and in the quality of our national life' (Heyworth, 1965: para. 170). Time has run its course. So, (a) how far has social science contributed to improvement (assuming it has taken place); then (b) what has been the Council's contribution to that social science?

After four decades, Claus Moser sidestepped the big question. He extolled advances in the range, quality, public acceptance and visible influence of social science, calling it a 'remarkable transformation' (Nicol, 2001: vi). Quantitatively, yes; but in what measure had the expansion of social science knowledge transformed the nation? How far did Council grants connect with outcomes – to institutional, policy or social change? Patricia Thomas had found little evidence of take-up during the Council's first decade and a half: 'If it were possible to compare the aspiration of researchers as set out in their applications for grants with the final outcome in terms of social change, the results would be depressing. Judged solely in those terms the exercise would seem to have failed' (Bulmer, 1987: 53). Even if the Council has causal responsibility (for either the transformation of social science or national improvement) it's necessarily shared, for example with the government's own statistical and social survey work and non-academic producers of knowledge, along with other funders of knowledge, including the foundations. In what proportion?

The counterfactual does not get us very far. Without the Council the quantum of knowledge – the data plus all those reams of reports, journal articles, chapters in collections and monographs and, at one remove from the commissioned research, the expertise and minds of social scientists – would probably have been less. But in that mix were think tankers, non-academic social researchers, consultants, in-house advisers. Sorting the science sheep from the research (defined eclectically) goats is well nigh impossible. Take a contemporary arena, risk and regulation. Among other initiatives, the ESRC backed the Centre for the Analysis of Risk and Regulation at the London School of Economics (http://www.lse.ac.uk/accounting/CARR/aboutUs/Home.aspx). Its director, Bridget Hutter, knows a lot, and is consulted by government (in the form, for example, of the Food Standards Agency). But the thinking that organisations – including government departments and agencies – do about risk is informed from multiple conduits. From consultants, regulators, 'common sense', shared matrices as well, potentially, as academic endeavour supported by the Council.

MEASURES OF SUCCESS?

A ready indicator of Heyworth's 'efficiency of the national economy' is GDP growth. One gauge is international comparison. But how sensibly to link the organisation or amount of social science knowledge in the usual comparator economies, such as Germany or Canada? If, in OECD league tables, the UK performance is middling, what, if anything, does that say about UK social science in general, let alone the specific contribution of the research council? Aggregate GDP is one thing, but how it is distributed has also to be weighed. Social scientists would jib at any suggestion they are responsible for changes in the Gini coefficient, but someone must ask the counterintuitive question: how can a society rich in self-knowledge of the kind produced by excellent social science become more unequal? The answer is: easily, as the past half-century of UK history shows.

Heyworth's second aspiration was improved 'quality of life'. Widen it to embrace sustainability, climate change and the environment. And trust in politics and institutions. Where is the value added from Council social science? Heyworth believed – a typically '60s view – that knowledge had therapeutic qualities. What he meant was that if planners, officials, business managers and other decision makers knew more, thanks to social science, they would make 'better' decisions and those dependent on them would benefit.

Quality of life is a value. Like 'dumbing down', it's impossible to measure change over time without imposing some absolute scheme, present and past. But schemes are built on norms, argued over in politics and culture, not science. Meanwhile, work by social scientists on gender, ethnicity, as well as sustainability has surely influenced the climate (of opinion) and culture. We don't have much to go on; social scientists have been relatively uninterested in tracing and modelling the processes by knowledge moves; research evaluation is under-developed (which helps explain the crudity of the REF 2014 impact procedures). Where, to complement the study of attitudes, is our grasp of underlying patterns in sensibility – such as the strengthening of individualism, and the decline of confidence in collective provision?

Social science has invested heavily in attitude surveys. They show that, in 2013, 17 per cent of the British Social Attitudes sample 'always' trusted governments, less than half 1986's level (Ormston and Curtice, 2015). The reasons may have to do with politics and parties during the past years, but the finding throws Heyworth's hope overboard. Social scientists may disclaim any responsibility, but in doing so advertise their marginality.

Perhaps Heyworth's criteria are too large. A subtler statement of purpose came from Andrew Shonfield. It was the generic desire, in the face of greatly accelerated change, to reduce the area of the unpredictable to a manageable series of clear alternatives (Shonfield, 1965). We can find out whether decision makers use social science – though there has been dismayingly little empirical investigation of the cognitive basis of institutional decision making. Academy schools, Universal Credit, the bedroom tax (to take some recent examples from the Cameron era) or (from the Labour years) foundation trusts in the NHS, the Private Finance Initiative, sundry changes to criminal justice, police and prisons …there is a long and open-ended list of policies from which evidence (defined as identifiable academic study) is missing. But of course those policies (like decisions made by businesses and organisations at large) are made by deploying knowledge – informal, ephemeral, Polanyi-esque.

THE POOL OF KNOWLEDGE, AGAIN

Specific examples such as those illustrate the problem of pinning down, let alone calibrating, Heyworth's suggestion that social science would 'repay' through improved policies. Social science knowledge exists as a cloud or, inverting the liquid metaphor, a pool into which economic and social actors (and the public and its intermediaries) may dip. Even if they do, the swim only leaves some flesh wet and the swimmer unable to recollect how or when it happened. But how shallow or deep? What criteria should determine the flow of resources both to social science and within social science? In practice they are internal and 'private' – a mix of incrementalism and demands from within disciplines to move along a self-defined knowledge trajectory.

Imagine if, alternatively, funding were geared to original purpose. The title of this book comes from a leader in *The Times* (long before its corruption by Rupert Murdoch) welcoming the Heyworth Report (*The Times*, 1965):

> There is no need to allow the more exaggerated claims made on behalf of the social sciences in order to agree that they are capable of making a far greater contribution to the good government and wise ordering of society than the paucity of their present resources permits.

That phrase 'good government' is telling. The 50-year relationship between social science and government as practice has been neither close nor cumulative. We lack, still, 'a strong and compelling evidence base documenting improvements in public services arising from increased research use' (Nutley et al., 2007: 298). Public service waned, waxed and is now waning again, often without any identifiable social science involvement, whether guiding the hand of ministers in making tax and spend decisions or adjusting institutions or deployed by officials in organising services and functions. The Council and the state's own agencies for audit, inspection and improvement have existed in non-communicating silos. The latter have done research but rarely deployed social science knowledge. The NAO investigates efficiency, effectiveness and economy without those categories stirring the loins of social researchers or the research council taking any ownership. Where it might have added value was in connecting the vast amount of data and analysis collected under the rubric of elections and public policy and delivery. Instead, election studies were undertaken in isolation. Perhaps voting has only contingent connexions with policy and public services – but that would be a finding worthy of much additional analysis and a lot more publicity.

A more cunning research council might, with the connivance of perspicacious social scientists, have sought knowledge of those mysterious recesses of government where power resides and critical decisions made, including decisions about science budgets. Such as the Treasury. The SSRC did support a classic study, carried out by Americans (Heclo and Wildavsky, 1974). But how many civil servants or ministers subsequently read it or changed their perceptions as a result? Of course it's not the fault of the Council if the British administrative class is unself-reflexive and avoids analysis. But if, after a half-century, the Treasury remains at the heart of Westminster as a structured impediment to good and effective government, don't we need to explain the persistence of the refusal of that informed self-consciousness, which after all is the object and ambition of social science as Lord Heyworth conceived it? Social science (and the Council) never quite got that the terrain of ideas was the site of ideological struggle. The political right did. Hayek and Friedman were exemplars of the Diceyan insight that ideas had 'generative capacity' and intellectual argument could transform political practice: 'their confidence in their ideological agency enabled them to exert it on a world historical stage' (Burgin, 2012: 222). This observation makes the 1970s and '80s critical decades. Social science did not realise the game being played; it was outmanoeuvred and surpassed. Technical debates are 'sometimes proxy wars between competing visions about the scale and scope of the state' (Hood et al., 2014: 15). During the recent financial crisis, the theory was advanced that above 90 per cent the debt/GDP ratio would retard growth. But this was shown to be based on unreliable data or, to put it unacademically, it was wrong.

Social science remains locked in the belief that knowledge is action. When the ESRC says the birth cohort studies *will* make a contribution to social and public health policy, what it means is that findings from the study *ought* to equip policy makers; if they knew more their decisions ought to have greater effect or 'stick'. The promotional material goes on to consider childhood obesity. Evidence from the Life Study will help formulate policies to improve food choice or increase physical activity among young children (ESRC, 2015b). Yes, but emphasis must be laid on 'help'. Other relevant evidence could be deployed, for example evidence about policy design and consequent effectiveness; the Life Study is unlikely in itself to offer much on how policies are to be paid for, 'sold' to public and media or implemented in any given fiscal or institutional circumstances.

Over the half-century much social science has found evidence of inequality. That is regrettable, researchers have implied, and, making a normative judgement, should be actionable. It is reasonable, and scientific, to show that forms and amounts of inequality are associated with costs and consequences. If since 1965 the UK has become less equal – in income, in the correlative strength of family background on life chances, longevity or morbidity – does that speak to some failure on the part of social science, or its research council? The founding generation would likely have counted it as failure.

In an odd book, an LSE economist examined psychology, economics, sociology and political science, looking especially at what they had to say in work published in the 1990s on a set of illustrative 'questions' such as the family, crime and money (Steuer, 2003). It's all the more remarkable for his willingness to step outside his discipline and make judgements on the intellectual quality of other social sciences. His verdict can be offered as an approximate assessment of 30 years of social science spending, though it may be noteworthy that his examination never once mentioned the Council. He is assertive, but a strain of dismay runs through the book. His bibliography cites some 250 works published from 1988 to 1998, of which 24 per cent originated from the UK, 66 per cent from the United States and 10 per cent from the rest of the world. (Does that say anything about the 'scientific quality' of UK social science – a proportion of which would have been directly or indirectly supported by the ESRC?) His ambiguous conclusion was that simultaneously social science had much to tell policy makers yet was silent on significant questions. On the business of securing the attention of policymakers – convoluted, frustrating, demanding patience, understanding and sympathy for politics – he was silent.

SNAPSHOT SOCIAL SCIENCE

Much social research is context bound. So research must necessarily be continuous and repetitive, not in the sense of repeating the same investigation but investigating a phenomenon that has changed in the intervening period. This bolsters the case for funding, but weakens analogies between the social and physical and life sciences, where the growth of knowledge is demonstrably cumulative. Adair Turner, the short-lived ESRC chair, notes that because beliefs and behaviour adapt to changes in environment there are few if any stable parameters or relationships in economics (Cassidy, 2009: 361). Good economics can help address problems and avoid specific risks and think through responses; it 'is never going to provide the certain simple and complete answers which the pre-crisis conventional wisdom appeared to'. How much of an indictment of the Council is it that conventional wisdom had been allowed to become conventional?

Yesterday's conclusions might have been appropriate to time and place; reality then changed. Social science forecasting has no great track record. Patterns discerned during one decade disappeared the next. 'The main shift in the growth pattern has been towards the medium and smaller size cities. Typically, in Britain, it is places like Leicester and Bristol that have gained population and places like Manchester, Liverpool and London that have lost people'

(Eversley, 1980: 8–9). In fact the trajectories of each of those places has been different, undermining generalisation, invalidating prediction. The urban analysts of the late 1970s were right that the free marketeers had won but wrong, up to a point, in seeing cities abandoned to market forces, millions living in deprivation and squalor amid yawning empty spaces (Eversley, 1980: 476). It wasn't that they were wrong on, say, the differential impact of what came to be called globalisation on cities; they just didn't see it coming. In 1980 'immigration' was classified under 'race'.

SOCIAL SCIENCE AND HISTORY

History shot our fox. Unpredicted by social scientists, changes in employment and economic relationships killed or evaporated the forces the social science story depended on for its credibility and public reputation. Among the transhistorical vehicles derailed by history was social class. Of course class remains a lens and a category of analysis. But 50 years ago social science could claim a lien on the future as the 'science of class'; you didn't have to be a Marxist to believe that class division was permanent and that the working class was an enduring majority. Few saw the decline of manufacturing, the weakening of solidarity between workers in 'objectively' similar pay and employment conditions, the triumph of a consumerist, individualist culture, mass immigration and so on. When they happened social scientists tried to understand. Explanations were retrofitted to circumstances.

In 1994 the OPCS commissioned the ESRC to review socio-economic classifications, and despite prevailing Tory and Labour sentiment, a revised version of the scheme developed in the 1970s by John Goldthorpe was adopted. Yet class as understood by the Goldthorpe generation was dying – class as an historical actor, an identifier or strongly causal factor in voting or job seeking. With it the spine of entire disciplines – notably sociology – crumbled. The Council stood by and watched as they in turn fragmented: gender and ethnicity and sexual orientation were sources of division, not unification.

It's a similar story with trade unions. Once the SSRC invested heavily in explicating and collecting data about institutions that were not just salient in contemporary politics but were regarded as a permanent part of conjuncture within firms, communities and the nation at large. The SSRC created a trade union research centre. The waters ebbed; the 'winter of discontent' (1978–9) was high tide. The retreat of unionism was shown by the ease with which a Tory peer, Lord Beloff (a social science academic), could successfully engineer an inquisition into the unit.

The SSRC was itself an emanation of belief in the benignity and necessity of the state, able to see in time, capable of moderating capitalism and improving people. The social science establishment was late in realising the pull of the Tory (and, later, Shirley Williams-ite) contention that social policy in the 1960s and 1970s had overreached itself and the political class started undermining itself by complaining the state was attempting to do too much. Some social scientists climbed on the bandwagon and 'overload' enjoyed a period of fashionableness. The Council responded, as it were, by ignoring the state, how it is constituted and managed. If the public sector has been beset by continuous reforms and 'modernisation' over the past three decades, both social science and the Council have been curiously absent.

The social sciences grew up thinking their vocation was to speak truth to power and that power resided in the state (Calhoun, 2014). But if the action moved away, to private companies or dispersed organisations, they were not geared up to follow. As the state itself became fragmented and differentiated, the Council could not keep up, losing track of where knowledge and decision making now intersected in schools, the NHS, contracting companies and transnational organisations.

THE PUBLIC

The Council has taken occasional steps to 'engage' the public; it now encourages grant holders to disseminate their work and offers media training as well as supporting a press office and, over the years, a suite of publications aimed at audiences beyond academe. On that basis the ESRC could be said to carry some responsibility for the public's general state of knowledge and enlightenment on economy and society.

Their enlightenment does not appear to go far. Post-2008 crisis research commissioned by the BBC Trust found the public saying they wanted information, but large numbers acknowledged their lack of understanding. The study registered complaints about 'economic jargon', which may include such everyday terms as credit, money, and probably does embrace GDP, central bank, and deficit (BBC Trust, 2012). 'Macroeconomics does not have the same kind of consensus now that applied before 2008 – economics is having its own crisis – and it could be difficult to conclude that a certain view was definitive or authoritative.' Academics had deep(er) knowledge 'but some also hold extreme views'. Where is the policing or standards-setting mechanism? Peer review palpably does not secure the best; Gresham's law may well apply.

Opinion polls do not always test cognitive capacity – respondents' command of facts, information or understanding. Views may be fact free. But our half-century question has to be: 'more or less' than before? How might the new knowledge and voluminous research have changed attitudes? A vignette on knowledge. Before launching its administrative data programme, the ESRC commissioned Ipsos Mori to conduct focus groups; it is, after all, the public's data. I attended one in a hotel on the outskirts of King's Lynn, divided between younger and older members of the public. The phrase 'administrative data' means little or nothing to the public (so the investigators found), but people do have views about both research and the propriety and utility of allowing easier access to health, local authority, criminal justice, school and similar data. Awareness of scientific method, statistics and data protection is low. People assumed the state already linked data and found it hard to understand why the Administrative Data Research Network was being launched. Participants tended to a pragmatic and public-spirited view: if the research produced benefit (usually defined as better public services) they didn't mind data exploitation. But there was a kind of deception going on. The examples Ipsos put up were about GPs and buses; in other words, giving a strongly instrumental, utilitarian push. The focus groups could not quite fathom what the ESRC was paying for unless it was 'useful' outputs, preferably to be fed back to specific places and services. The public would hesitate to make a hard and fast distinction between consultancy and research or between research carried out, say, by Norfolk County Council and by the University of East Anglia. What went on in universities beyond teaching students was mysterious, though the concept of a laboratory had purchase. They found it hard to justify this kind of knowledge ever being 'for its own sake' or for developing theory. If those focus group findings are generalisable, 50 years have done little to educate the public in the purposes of socio-economic research, as conceived by academics at least.

CONCLUSION

The past half-century has seen the rise of markets and the preponderant influence of American models in organising firms and public bodies, and declining faith in the state, certainly of the fervour around when the SSRC was born. Market liberalism despises politics for its myopia, instability and selfishness, believing free markets avoid such frailties (Roberts, 2010). The financial crisis disproved this thoroughly, leaving social science in today's limbo. Given the present state of social science knowledge, we should recognise how conflicting and uncertain its interpretations are – which was Martin Rein's verdict in 1976, and 40 years on still holds (Rein, 1976: 33).

You are misreading social science as policy science, it might be said. But policy is the fate of social science. Aaron Wildavsky sagely wrote that if power is in pieces, which resist picking up, and truth is partial, resistant to being made whole, what is the point of seeking to contribute to policy? Turn the point round, he said: if power were unitary and knowledge were perfect, the analysis (social science) would either be supreme (because it's right) or superfluous, because there are no errors to correct (Wildavsky, 1979: 405–6).

There are no solutions. Social scientists can think about alternatives to what is. In their professional capacity they have better opportunities than anyone else enjoys to try to narrow the widening gap between the causal and moral complexity of the predicaments with which all modern political communities are confronted and the causal and moral adequacy of the understanding which they can collectively bring to bear (Dunn, 1990: 212–13).

> Social scientists regularly complain about the mindset they encounter in Westminster and Whitehall that demands answers. But they are reluctant themselves to convince the public of any alternative. At best, this is the promise of a rich, explanatory narrative that will take time and money (and longitudinal surveys) to compile. At worst, it is a crude rejection of existing politics and a utopian insistence that things be different – but meanwhile let the taxpayer pay. (Walker, 2001)

PROBLEM SOLVERS, NOT SCIENTISTS

If you do policy work you are enmeshed in values. David Eversley recalled the Roskill Commission on the third London airport. 'Social science found Cublington … value-judgements and unquantified philosophies about the environment added to intuitions about regional planning found Foulness' (Bulmer, 1978: 298). This is characteristic of the Open Society. Its enemies would deliver us to the mercies of the model-makers, the survey analysts and the linear programmers

Was the balance got right between the 'pure' side of the study of behaviour and applicability? I can only repeat the judgement made over 60 years ago by Ithiel de Sola Poole: 'more social scientists inside and outside of university [should] play the role of problem solvers rather than scientific discoverers' (cited in Rein, 1976: 58) or, put in terms of this history, the organisers and strategists of social science (the Council) should have thought a lot more and a lot harder about the respective volumes and integration of problem-oriented work, data and infrastructure and – necessarily a small proportion of the total – social science with no obvious bearing on today and today's issues. 'It matters not at all whether what we're doing counts as social policy or social administration or sociology, whether it belongs in the field of education or health or welfare or in public policy. The questions override territorial enclosures' (Oakley, 2014: 258).

Applicability cuts across traditional disciplinary boundaries. Any 'solution' drawn from a single discipline is likely to be wrong. Any policy decision involves economic, social, political, legal and administrative knowledge and knowledge of the subject matter (Hogwood and Peters, 1985: 21). But that knowledge will be bitty, marginal, a mélange. In education (let's extend the domain to include research) we confront great tracts of practice – what children experience at school – that is not uninflected by social science knowledge but touched in a glancing, contingent, unpredictable way (or not at all). Teachers complain of low quality evidence, not enough evidence, lack of context specific evidence, lack of funding to support inset (in-service training) days and – killer punch – 'the low credibility of the academics who produce evidence' (Shepherd, 2014: 26). If that perception is accurately reported, whose responsibility is it to improve the reputation of social science academics? If it is just, 50 years of Council activity in education have failed.

A PLEA FOR MODESTY

We must avoid a promissory story, while acknowledging that past knowledge can be useful (Prewitt, 2015). We are creating a store of knowledge. We have to come up with a more complex story about what we do, protecting 'space' (autonomy) for thought, reflection and theory. But as Prewitt had the courage to admit, this space may have to be smaller, fiscally defensible, acknowledging that more does not necessarily mean better.

In the broader field of social research, it's time to recapitulate what Andrew Shonfield, the greatest of Council chairs, realised early on. Social science research tends to produce useful ideas with an increasingly factual base rather than definitive answers to major policy questions (SSRC, 1971). No set of firm generalisations will emerge from research that the policy maker will be able blindly to apply. She will still need plenty of judgement … but will have a much stronger basis of factual material to judge by. The ultimate pay-off from this type of work is that no one's intuitive powers will have to be stretched to excessive lengths.

REFERENCES

Alsop, A. 1999. The RAE and the production of knowledge, *History of the Human Sciences*, 12: 116–120.

Bacon, R. and Eltis, W. 1976. *Britain's Economic Problem: Too few producers*. London: Macmillan.

Barber, M. 2015. *How to Run A Government So That Citizens Benefits and Taxpayers Don't Go Crazy*. London: Allen Lane.

Barker, P. 1972. *A Sociological Portrait*. London: Penguin.

BBC Trust, 2012. Seminar on Impartiality and Economic Reporting, 6 November.

Bell, D. 1972. The Cultural Contradictions of Capitalism. New York: Basic Books.

Binmore, K. 2003. In Steuer, M. *The Scientific Study of Society*. Boston, MA: Kluwer.

BIS (Department for Business, Innovation and Skills) 2010. The Allocation of Science and Research Funding 2011/12 to 2014/15. December.

BIS (Department for Business, Innovation and Skills) 2013. A Strategy for Future Retail. October.

BIS (Department for Business, Innovation and Skills) 2014. The Allocation of Science and Research Funding 2015/16. May.

BIS (Department for Business, Innovation and Skills) 2014b. 7th Survey of Knowledge Transfer Activities – PSREs and Research Councils. July.

Blume, S. 1987. Social science in Whitehall: two analytic perspectives in Bulmer, M. (ed.) *Social Science Research and Government*. Cambridge: Cambridge University Press.

Blunkett, D. 2000. Influence or irrelevance: can social science improve government? ESRC lecture February. *Research Intelligence*, 71: 12–21.

Boyle, P. n.d. Understanding the third sector – the work of the Third Sector Research Centre 2008–2013, University of Birmingham.

British Academy, 2008. Punching our weight: the humanities and social sciences in public policy making. September.

British Academy, 2015. State of the nation: a review of evidence on the supply and demand of quantitative skills. June.

Brown, M. and Madge, N. 1982. *Despite the Welfare State*. A report on the SSRC/DHSS programme of research into transmitted deprivation. London: Heinemann.

BSA, HaPS, ESRC. 2010. British Sociological Association, Heads and Professors of Sociology Group, ESRC International Benchmarking Review of UK Sociology.

BSA. 2014. 'ESRC Consultation' response by British Sociological Association and Council of Heads and Professors of Sociology.

Bulmer, M. 1978. 'Social science research and policy-making in Britain' in Bulmer, M. (ed.) *Social Policy Research*. London: Macmillan.

Bulmer, M. 1985. The influence of research on policy: how do they relate? *Research Policy and Planning* 3, 2.

Bulmer, M. (ed.) 1987. *Social Science Research and Government: Comparative Essays on Britain and the United States*. Cambridge: Cambridge University Press.

Bulmer, M. 1996. Are university departments research organisations? *Bulletin de Méthodologie Sociologique*, 50: 84–92.

Burgess, S. 2014. 'The London Effect' in Britain in 2015. ESRC.

Burgin, A. 2012. *The Great Persuasion: Reinventing free markets since the depression*. Boston, MA: Harvard.

Butler, D., Adonis, A. and Travers, T. 1994. *Failure in British Government: Politics of the poll tax*. Oxford: Oxford University Press.

Cabinet Office, 2012. Open Data White Paper June, Cm 8353, par 2.67.

Calhoun, C. 2014. Campaign for Social Science. Annual Lecture. https://campaignforsocialscience.org.uk/news/glass-half-full-social-science-campaign-annual-lecture-hears/

Carter, C. (ed.) 1981. *Industrial Policy and Innovation*. London: Heinemann.

CASE (Centre for the Analysis of Social Exclusion, LSE), 2015. The Coalition's Record on the Under Fives: Policy, Spending and Outcomes, 2010–2015.

Cassidy, J. 2009. *How Markets Fail*. London: Penguin.

Challis, L. et al. 1988. *Joint Approaches to Social Policy*. Cambridge: Cambridge University Press.

Cherns, A. 1972. Introduction, in Cherns, A., Sinclair, R., Jenkins, W. (eds) *Social Science and Government: Policies and problems*. London: Tavistock.

Cherns, A. 1979. *Using the Social Sciences*. London: Routledge & Kegan Paul.

Cherns, A. and Perry, N. 1976. The development and structure of social science research in Britain, in Crawford, E. and Perry, N. (eds) *Demands for Social Knowledge: The role of research organizations*. Beverly Hills, CA: SAGE.

Clapham Committee Report, 1946. Provision for Social and Economic Research Cmnd 6868, HMSO.

Commission on the Social Sciences, 2003. Great expectations: the social sciences in Britain, Academy of Learned Societies for the Social Sciences.

CPRS, 1971. Central Policy Review Staff. A Framework for Government Research and Development, Cmnd 4814, London: HMSO.

Crawford, E. and Perry, N. (eds) 1976. *Demands for Social Knowledge: The role of research organizations*. Beverly Hills, CA: Sage.

Crosland, A. 1975. Foreword, *SSRC Newsletter*, 26 February.

Curtice, J. 2002. Survey research and electoral change in Britain. Centre for Research into Elections and Social Trends Working Paper 96, March.

Dahrendorf, R. 1995a. Whither Social Sciences? The 6th ESRC Annual Lecture.

Dahrendorf, R. 1995b. LSE Oxford.

Davies, W. 2015. ESRC Alpha Territory Project, LSE Seminar, Elites and urban dynamics, 22 July.

Desai, M. 2015. *Hubris: Why economists failed to predict the crisis and how to avoid the next one*. London: Yale University Press.

Donnison, D. 1978. 'Research for Policy', in Bulmer, M. (ed.) *Social Policy Research*. London: Macmillan.

Donovan, C. 2001. Government policy and the direction of social science research. PhD thesis, University of Sussex, November.

Duncan, S. 2015. Personal communication.

Dunn, J. 1990. *Interpreting Political Responsibility*. Cambridge: Polity Press.

Dunn, J. 2000. *The Cunning of Unreason: Making sense of politics*. London: HarperCollins.

DWP (Department of Work and Pensions) 2003. Evaluation of the New Deal for Lone Parents, Working Age Report 146.

ESRC, 1989. Urban and regional change in the 1980s. http://www.esrc.ac.uk/

ESRC, 1990. Social Sciences Issue 7, October.

ESRC, 2004a. Operating report 2003–2004. http://www.esrc.ac.uk/

ESRC, 2004b. Seven ages of man and woman. A look at life in Britain in the second Elizabethan era. http://www.esrc.ac.uk/

ESRC, 2008. The edge, Spring. http://www.esrc.ac.uk/

ESRC, 2009. Britain in 2010. http://www.esrc.ac.uk/

ESRC, 2010. Britain in 2011. http://www.esrc.ac.uk/

ESRC, 2013a. Evaluation Committee Annual Report 2012. June. http://www.esrc.ac.uk/

ESRC, 2013b. External Communications Plan 2011–2014 Annex 1. http://www.esrc.ac.uk/

ESRC, 2013c. Global summit for retail and researchers. http://www.esrc.ac.uk/

ESRC, 2013d. http://www.esrc.ac.uk/

ESRC, 2014a. Press Release, The changing face of the high street. http://www.esrc.ac.uk/

ESRC, 2014b. Delivery plan 2015–2016. http://www.esrc.ac.uk/

ESRC, 2015a. Strategic plan. http://www.esrc.ac.uk/

ESRC, 2015b. Life style study. http://www.esrc.ac.uk/

ESRC, 2015c. Annual Report and Accounts 2014–15. http://www.esrc.ac.uk/

ESRC, 2015d. *Society Now*, Summer 2015. Issue 22. http://www.esrc.ac.uk/

Eversley, D. 1978. 'A question of numbers?', in Bulmer, M. (ed.) *Social Science Research and Government: Comparative Essays on Britain and the United States*. Cambridge: Cambridge University Press.

Eversley, D. 1980. 'A planner's perspective', in Evans, A. and Eversley, D. (eds) *The Inner City Employment and Industry*. London: Heinemann Educational Books for the CES.

Evidence Briefing n.d. http://www.esrc.ac.uk/

Flather, P. 1987. 'Pulling through: Conspiracies, counterplots and how the SSRC escaped the axe', in Bulmer, M. (ed.) *Social Science Research and Government: Comparative Essays on Britain and the United States*. Cambridge: Cambridge University Press.

Fulton Report, 1968. Report of the Committee chaired by Lord Fulton: The Civil Service, Cmnd 3638.

Gibbons, M. et al. 1994. *The New Production of Knowledge*. London: Sage.

Gillespie, A. 2010. *Society Now*, Spring.

Goldthorpe, J. 1980. *Social Mobility and Class Structure in Modern Britain*. Oxford: Clarendon Press.

Gregg, P. and Machin, S. 1998. Childhood disadvantage and success or failure in the youth labour. Centre for Economic Performance, Discussion Paper 397.

Greer, P. 1994. *Transforming Central Government*. Buckingham: Open University Press.

Guardian, 2010. http://www.theguardian.com/politics/2010/dec/19/coalition-gov ernment-chaos-theory-politics

Hallsworth, M. and Rutter, J. 2011. Making Policy Better: Improving Whitehall's core business. *Institute for Government*, April.

Halsey, A. H. 2004. *A History of Sociology in Britain*. Oxford: Oxford University Press.

Hammersley, M. (ed.) 2002. *Educational Research: Policymaking and Practice*. London: Sage.

Hammersley, M. 2015. *Times Higher Education*, 5 February, p. 31.

Hargreaves, D. 1996. Teaching as a research-based profession. The Teaching Training Agency, Annual Lecture.

Harloe, M. n.d. Some fulfilment of a lifetime's ambition. Quoting from: Peter Townsend's 1979 *Poverty in the UK*. London: Penguin.

Haslam, C. and Bryman, A. (eds) 1994. *Social Scientists Meet the Media*. London: Routledge.

Hay, C. 2007. *Why We Hate Politics* Cambridge: Polity Press.

Heald, G. 1990. Viewpoint, *Social Sciences*, Issue 7, October.

Heclo, H. and Wildavsky, A. 1974. *The Private Government of Public Money*. Berkeley and Los Angeles: The University of California Press.

Hennessy, P. (ed.) 2007. *The New Protective State*. London: Continuum.

Heyworth, G. 1965. Heyworth Committee Report of the Committee on Social Studies, Cmnd 2660.

Hills, J. 2014. *Good Times, Bad Times: The welfare myth of them and us*. Bristol: Policy Press.

HM Treasury, 2011. The Magenta Book. Guidance for Evaluation, April.

HM Treasury, 2015. A country that lives within its means. Cmnd 9112, July.

Hogwood, B. W. and Peters, B. G. 1985. *The Pathology of Public Policy*. Oxford: Oxford University Press.

Hood, C. and Dixon, R. 2015. *A Government that Worked Better and Cost Less?* Oxford: Oxford University Press.

Hood, C., Heald, D. and Himaz, R. (eds) 2014. *When the Party's Over: The politics of fiscal squeeze in perspective*. London: British Academy.

Hope, K. 1978. Indicators of the State of Society, in Bulmer, M. (ed.) *Social Policy Research*. London: Macmillan.

House of Commons Library, 2015. http://researchbriefings.parliament.uk/Research Briefing/Summary/CBP-7257#fullreport

Howson, S. 2011. *Lionel Robbins*. Cambridge: Cambridge University Press.

Impact Case Study (REF 3b). UoA2 family and gender role change. University of Cambridge.

Ince, M. 2015. A question of economics, *Society Now*, Summer, Issue 22.

Institute for Government, 2015. Select Committees under scrutiny, June.

ISER n.d. a. Institute for Social and Economic Research. Taking the long view 2013–2014.

ISER n.d. b. Institute for Social and Economic Research. Taking the long view 2014–2015.

IUS Committee, 2009. House of Commons Innovation, Universities, Science and Skills Committee Putting science and engineering at the heart of government policy 8th report

Jarvis, M. 2005. *Conservative Governments: Morality and social change in affluent Britain 1957–64*. Manchester: Manchester University Press.

Jones, K. 1988. Fifty years of economic research. *National Institute Economic Review*, 128: 36–59.

JRF, 2014. Joseph Rowntree Foundation: Reducing Poverty in the UK: A Collection of Evidence Reviews, August.

Kay, J. 2015. What is the good company? *Social Europe*, 17 August. http://www.socialeurope.eu/2015/08/what-is-the-good-company/

Kaysen, C. 1968. Model makers and decision makers: Economist and the policy process, *Public Interest*, No. 12, Summer.

Keeble, D. 1998. Local industrial development and dynamics: the East Anglian case. ESRC Centre for Business Research, Working Paper 96, June.

King, A. and Crewe, I. 2013. *The Blunders of our Governments*. London: Oneworld.

Kogan, M. and Henkel, M. 2000. 'Future directions for higher education policy research', in Schwartz, S. and Teichler, U. (eds) *The Institutional Basis of Higher Education Research*. New York: Kluwer.

Lansley, S. and Mack, J. 2015. *Breadline Britain: The rise of mass poverty*. London: Oneworld.

Lenihan, A. 2013. Lessons from abroad. International approaches to promoting evidence-based social policy, Alliance for Useful Evidence, July.

Lewis, J. n.d. The fluctuating fortunes of the social sciences since 1945, unpublished paper submitted to Commission on the Social Sciences 2003.

LGA, 2015. Local Government Association, Centre for Population Change. Local Government and the Demography of Ageing, March.

Lindblom, C. 1980. *The Policy Making Process*. New York: Prentice Hall.

Lowndes, V. and McCaughie, K. 2013. Weathering the perfect storm? Austerity and institutional resilience in local government. *Policy & Politics*, 41 (4): 533–549.

Lunn, P. 2014. *Regulatory Policy and Behavioural Economics*. OECD Publishing. (http://www.keepeek.com/Digital-Asset-Management/oecd/governance/regulatory-policy-and-behavioural-economics_9789264207851-en#page3).

Lynd, R. 1939. *Knowledge for What?* Princeton: Princeton University Press.

Martin, B. 2011. The research excellence framework and the 'impact agenda': are we creating a Frankenstein monster? *Research Evaluation* 20 (3), September: 247–254.

Matthews, R. 1990. '25 years of the ESRC'. *Social Sciences*, October, Issue 7.

Mitchell, J. 1968. Foreword to Research in Political Science, *SSRC Review*, cited in Cherns, A. 1975 On economics and social sciences in Britain, *Révue Economique*, 26 (6): 1025.

MRC, 2014. Maximising the value of UK population cohorts. March. London: Medical Research Council.

NAO, 2013. Cross-government evaluation in government. December. National Audit Office.

Nathan, R. 1988. *Social Science in Government. Uses and misuses.* New York: Basic Books.

Newby, H. 1990. *Social Sciences,* Issue 7. ESRC.

New Society, 1984. 1 March.

Nicol, A. 2001. *The Social Sciences Arrive.* ESRC. http://www.esrc.ac.uk/

Nutley, S., Walter, I. and Davies, H. 2007. *Using Evidence.* Bristol: Policy Press.

Oakley, A. 2014. *Father and Daughter. Patriarchy: Gender and social science.* Bristol: Policy Press.

O'Hara, G. 2007. *From Dreams to Disillusionment: Economic and social planning in 1960s Britain.* London: Macmillan.

Ormston, R. and Curtice, J. (eds) 2015. British Social Attitudes: 32nd Report. London: NatCen. http://www.bsa.natcen.ac.uk/

Overman, H. 2015. The economic performance of UK cities. Centre for Economic Performance Paper, EA025.

PASC, 2012. House of Commons Public Administration Select Committee Strategic thinking in government, 24th Report, HC 1625, April.

PEP, 1966. *Political and Economic Planning, Attitudes in British Management.* London. Penguin.

Perry, N. 1976. Research settings in the social sciences: a re-examination, in Crawford, E. and Perry, N. (eds) *Demands for Social Knowledge: The role of research organizations.* Beverly Hills, CA: SAGE.

Platt, J. 2003. *The British Sociological Association. A sociological history.* BSA Sociology Press.

Posner, M. 1982. Preface to Brown, M. and Madge, N. *Despite the Welfare State.* London: Heinemann.

Prewitt, K. 2015. Presentation at Strategic Forum for the Social Sciences, July.

Quirk, B. 2015. *High performing councils: Recipe not alchemy.* Public Policy Institute for Wales, July.

Rein, M. 1976. *Social Science and Public Policy.* London: Penguin.

Reinhart, C. and Rogoff, K. 2009. *This Time is Different: Eight centuries of financial folly.* Princeton: Princeton University Press.

Rex, J. 1973. Quoted in Holmwood, J. and Scott, J. (eds) 2014. *The Palgrave Handbook of Sociology in Britain.* London: Palgrave. p. 402.

Riecken, H.W. 1969. Social sciences and social problems, *Social Science Information* 8 (1): 101–129.

Roberts, A. 2010. *The Logic of Discipline: Global capitalism and the architecture of government.* Oxford: Oxford University Press.

Robinson, A. and Sandford, C. 1983. *Tax Policy Making in the UK.* London: Heinemann.

Rothschild, N.M.V. 1982. Lord Rothschild's Enquiry into the Social Science Research Council, Cmnd 8554, HMSO.

Science and Technology Committee, 2012. House of Commons Science and Technology Committee. The Census and social science. Third Report of session 2012–2013, September.

Seabrook, J. 2013. *Pauperland: Poverty and the poor in Britain.* London: C. Hurst & Co.

Shepherd, J. 2014. How to achieve more effective services: the evidence eco system. What Works Network, Cardiff University.

Shonfield A. 1965. *Modern Capitalism*. Oxford: Oxford University Press.

Shonfield, A. 1972a. 'Research and public policy', in Cherns, A., Sinclair, R., Jenkins W. (eds) *Social Science and Government: Policies and problems*. London: Tavistock.

Shonfield, A. 1972b. The Social Sciences in the Great Debate on Science Policy. *Minerva X*, No. 3, July.

Shonfield, A. 1975. *SSRC Newsletter*, 29, November.

Shonfield, A. 1981. Does government have a role?, in Carter, C. (ed.) *Industrial Policy and Innovation*. London: Heinemann.

Silver, H. and Silver, P. 1992. War, skirmish or feint? Education against poverty 1960–1980, *British Journal of Sociology of Education*, 13 (4): 465–474.

Snow, C. (Lord) 1965. House of Lords debates, 18 November, vol. 270, col. 701.

SSRC, 1968. *Research in Political Science*. London: Heinemann.

SSRC, 1971. Annual Report 1970–1971.

SSRC, 1976. Social Science Research Council, Annual Report 1975–1976, p. 17.

Stanko, E. 2006. Theorizing about violence. *Violence Against Women*, 12 (6): 543–555.

Steuer, M. 2003. *The Scientific Study of Society*. Boston, MA: Kluwer.

Stewart, H. 2010. The Chair, the city and the case for research, *Society Now*, Spring, Issue 6.

Talbot, C. and Talbot, C. 2014. *Sir Humphrey and the Professors: What does Whitehall want from academic?* Manchester: University of Manchester.

The Times, 1965, Leader column, 3 June.

Thomas, P. 1985. *The Aims and Outcomes of Social Policy Research*. London: Croom Helm.

Townsend, P. 1979. *Poverty in the UK*. London: Penguin.

Toynbee, P. and Walker, D. 2010. *The Verdict. Did Labour change Britain?* London: Granta.

Toynbee, P. and Walker, D. 2015. *Cameron's Coup: How the Tories took Britain to the brink*. London: Guardian Faber Publishing.

Trist, E. 1972. Types of output mix of research organizations, in Cherns, A., Sinclair, R., Jenkins W. (eds) *Social Science and Government: Policies and problems*. London: Tavistock.

University of Leeds, 2012. http://www.sociology.leeds.ac.uk/assets/files/research/Regulatory_Dance/ImpactReportFinalDec2012.pdf

Vaitilingam, R. 2010. Recession Britain: findings from economic and social research. Undated ESRC.

Walker, D. 1975a. A man able to keep the balance, *Times Higher Education Supplement*, 25 July.

Walker, D. 1975b. SSRC doubts and uncertainties 10 years on, *Times Higher Education Supplement*, 5 December.

Walker, D. 1975c. *Times Higher Education*, 4 April.

Walker, D. 2001. *Times Higher Education*. 14 December, p. 33.

Walker, D. 2002. *Times Higher Education*. 7 September, p. 25.

Walker, D. 2015. Accounting for Hodge. *Public Money & Management*, 35 (3): May.

Wallerstein, I. et al. 1996. *Open the Social Sciences*. Report of the Gulbenkian Commission, Stanford University Press.

White Paper, 1993. Realising our potential: a strategy for science, engineering and technology, Cmnd 2250.

Wildavksy, A. 1979. *The Art and Craft of Policy Analysis*. London. Macmillan.

Wilsdon, J. et al. 2015. The Metric Tide. Report of the Independent Review of the Role of Metrics in Research Assessment and Management, Hefce, July.

Wilson, A. 2010. *Knowledge Power*. London: Routledge.

Wilson, W.J. 2002. Expanding the domain of policy-relevant scholarship in the social sciences, CASE paper 52, London School of Economics.

Witherspoon, S. 2015. Personal communication.

Young, M. (ed.) 1968. *Forecasting and the Social Sciences*. London: Heinemann.

Young, M. 1975. *SSRC Newsletter*, 29, November.

INDEX

academic capture 71
  academic freedom 79–80
  dirigisme 71–3
    defeated 75–6
  doctrine of curiosity 77–8
  in-house research 73–5
  trajectories of disciplines 80–2
Academic Liaison Officers (ALO) 40
accountability 63–4
agent of amelioration 59–60
  50 years of knowledge 67–70
  forecasting and 'span of control'
    60–2
  impact as accountability 63–4
  influence is normative 64–6
  politics and policy 66–7
  pool of knowledge 62–3
Amann, R. 57
antinomian knowledge 5–7
autistic knowledge 10–12

Barber, M. 96–7
Barker, P. 80, 81, 89, 93
Bartholomew, R. 12
behavioural economics 87
belief impervious to knowledge 89, 90
Blair government 53, 55–6, 57–8, 67
Blume, S. 49
Blunkett, D. 55–6, 57, 79
British Attitude Surveys 100
British Sociological Association (BSA) 7,
  75, 81, 100
Bulmer, M. 9, 41–2, 43, 45, 46–7, 64,
  73, 75, 78, 98–9, 107
Burgin, A. 102
business 15, 27, 34
  and management 96–7

Business Innovation and Skills (BIS),
  Department for 5, 17, 19, 21, 22,
  23, 26, 31, 72

Cabinet Office 21, 31, 33, 34,
  40, 56
Cameron governments 22, 43
  coalition 5, 22, 24, 33, 76, 88
causal formula 55–6
Central Policy Review Staff (CPRS)
  9, 42
Central Statistical Office 42, 43
Challis, L. et al. 8, 59
Cherns, A. 4–5, 7, 11, 27, 28, 37, 61
  and Perry, N. 74
Civil Service College 56, 75
civil society 88
Clapham Committee 38–9, 79
Commission on the Social Sciences
  3, 6
commissioner role 24–5
constitutional role
  democracy 19–20
  quango 20–3
corporate sector *see* business
Crosland, T. 60, 62
cumulative knowledge 83–5
  and belief 89, 90
  disconnect 89–91
  does it make a difference? 91–2
  economics 85–7
  education research 92–5
  and policy, relationship between
    87–8
  and public management 95–7
curiosity-driven research 77–8
Curtice, J. 92

Dahrendorf, R. 44, 71, 72, 81
data
    Big Data programmes 35
    UK Data Service/Survey Archive 28–9,
        74, 91–2
decentralisation 51–2
democracy 19–20
Desai, M. 87
Diamond, I. 50, 57, 86
disciplines, trajectories of 80–2
Donnison, D. 45, 75
Donovan, C. 72–3
Dunn, J. 66–7

economics 17–18, 80, 84, 85–7, 99, 105
education research 92–5, 108
Elliott, J. 36
election studies 92, 101
epistemological hierarchy 18–19, 94
ESRC today 16–19
    commissioner role 24–5
    and constitution 19–23
    policy evaluation and strategic research
        33–5
    science policy 23–4
    social science system and capacity 26–9
    strategic knowledge 29–30
    under the Tories 30–3
    and universities 25–6
ethnic relations research 74–5
Eversley, D. 82, 89, 103–4, 107
evidence 64–5

forecasting and 'span of control' 60–2
Fulton Report 40
funding/grants 1, 2–3, 4, 71–2
    applications 25–6
    as capital investment 31
    education 93
    IFS 76
    impact criterion 30
    and Secondary Data Analysis Initiative
        77–8
    and volunteering 88

Gibbons, M. et al. 2
Gillespie, A. 86
Goldthorpe, J. 73, 104
grants see funding/grants

Hague, D. 49, 52
Haldane principle 24
Halsey, A.H. 41, 44, 62, 73, 75, 81
Hammersley, M. 26, 45, 79–80
Heyworth Committee 4–5, 11, 37, 40,
        59, 61, 68, 73, 98, 99–101
Hills, J. 9, 90
historical perspective
    assassination 44–7
        counterfactual 47–8
    early years 39–41
    origins and destinations 38–9
    picture by 1975 41–4
    promise and disappointment 36–8
    and social science 104–5
Hogwood, B.W. and Peters, B.G.
        50–1, 108
Hood, C. et al. 102
Hope, K. 81

impact
    as accountability 63–4
    and research funding 30
in-house research 73–5
Ince, M. 83, 84
independent research organisations
        27–8, 76
inequality 102
    poverty studies 89, 90–1
Institute for Fiscal Studies (IFS) 14, 21,
        76, 84
Institute for Social and Economic
        Research (ISER) 23, 50, 85
invisibility of ESRC 8–10

Johnson, P. 84, 90
Joint Approach to Social Policy (JASP) 8
Joseph, K. 45–7, 60

Kay, J. 15
Kaysen, C. 59
Keeble, D. 95
knowledge 1–3, 13–15
    50 years of 67–70
    antinomian 5–7
    autistic 10–12
    epistemological hierarchy 18–19, 94
    growth of 4–5
    integration and utilisation 65–6

knowledge *cont.*
  pool of 62–3, 100–3
  state 16–19
  see also cumulative knowledge;
      strategic knowledge/research

Lansley, S. and Mack, J. 90
Letwin, O. 33, 46
Lewis, Janet 9
Lewis, J. 61
life course studies 69–70, 102
local knowledge 65–6
Lowndes, V. and McCaughie, K. 95

Magenta Book (HM Treasury) 6
Marshall, G. 57
Martin, B. 63
Matthews, R. 40, 77
Maude, F. 21, 31
measures of success 99–100
media 19, 92
Medical Research Council 23, 31, 68, 73–4
missed opportunities 57–8
Mitchell, J. 40
Moser, C. 7, 22, 65, 84, 98

Nathan, R. 1, 80
National Audit Office (NAO) 20, 33, 69
new public management 42, 51, 72
Newby, H. 49, 50, 52, 53, 62–3
Next Steps programme 51
Nicol, A. 36, 38, 84, 98
Nurse, P. 17, 18, 23–4, 31
Nutley, S. 101

Oakley, A. 108
Office of Budget Responsibility 76
Office of National Statistics (ONS) 22–3,
    51–2
opinion polls 12, 19, 106
Osborne, G. 10, 63, 85–6
Overman, H. 68

peer reviews 81
Pickles, E. 46, 90
Pissarides, C. 83, 84
policy
  evaluation and strategic research 33–5
  'policy for knowledge' 18, 24

policy *cont.*
  and politics 66–7
  science 23–4
  and social science research/knowledge,
      relationship between 87–8, 107–8
Posner, M. 46, 75
poverty studies 89, 90–1
problem-solver role 107–8
public engagement 105–6
'public sector research establishments' 23
public services 101
publicly funded research 63

'quality of life' improvement 99–100
quango 20–3
quantitative skills deficit 29, 82
Quirk, B. 96

Rein, M. 107
reprieve and normalisation 49–53
  causal formula 55–6
  missed opportunities 57–8
  reorganisation and thematic priorities
      53–4
  state modernisation and reform
      54–5
Research Councils UK (RCUK) 17, 18
Research Excellence Framework (REF) 18,
    63–4, 66, 79
research funding *see* funding/grants
'research initiative boards' 77
Rex, J. 74
Rieken, H.W. 81
Rothschild, Lord 42, 46, 47

science policy 23–4
Science and Technology Committee
    12, 23
Scottish independence 32
Secondary Data Analysis Initiative
    77–8
Shonfield, A. 39, 40, 42, 45, 70, 73, 79,
    80, 100, 108
snapshot social science 89, 103–4
Snow, Lord 98
social mobility studies 72–3
social science
  capacity 28–9
  and history 104–5

social science *cont.*
  and policy, relationship between 87–8,
    107–8
  research 7–8, 12–13
  snapshot 89, 103–4
  system 26–8
  see also knowledge
'span of control', forecasting and 60–2
state
  control 71–3
    defeated 75–6
  funding and volunteering 88
  knowledge 16–19
  modernisation and reform 54–5
Steuer, M. 103
Stewart, H. 86
strategic knowledge/research 29–30,
  39–40, 79
  policy evaluation and 33–5
Sure Start 9
Survey Archive/UK Data Service 28–9,
  74, 91–2
systematic reviews 84–5

Thatcher government 44–7
  counterfactual 47–8
thematic priorities 53–4
Third Sector Research Centre (TSRC)
  87–8
Thomas, P. 40, 43, 62, 78, 98–9

Tories 30–3, 34, 51, 53, 54–5
  see also Cameron governments;
    Thatcher government
Townsend, P. 90–1
Toynbee, P. and Walker, D. 22, 56
Treasury 20, 21, 101–2
  Magenta Book 6
  spending review (2015) 10
Trist, E. 79
Turner, A. 52, 103

UK Data Service/Survey Archive 28–9,
  74, 91–2
UK Statistics Authority 23, 69
universities 1–2, 4, 25–6, 74, 75, 78, 106
  Scottish 32

volunteering 88

Walker, D. 56, 73, 75
  Toynbee, P. and 22, 56
Whitaker, T. 52
Wildavsky, A. 107
Willets, D. 10, 22
Williams, S. 8, 42–3
Wilson, A. 65
Wilson, R. 57
Wilson government 8, 41, 60, 68, 98

Young, M. 10, 40, 60–2, 73–4, 79, 86